Norwich

Above: Guildhall Hill from the market place.

Right: Pleasure wherry 'Hathor' at Pull's Ferry.

Below: Coslany Street towards St Miles.

ENGLISH CITY COMPANION

Norwich

Michael Gibbs
Photographs by Michael Adcock

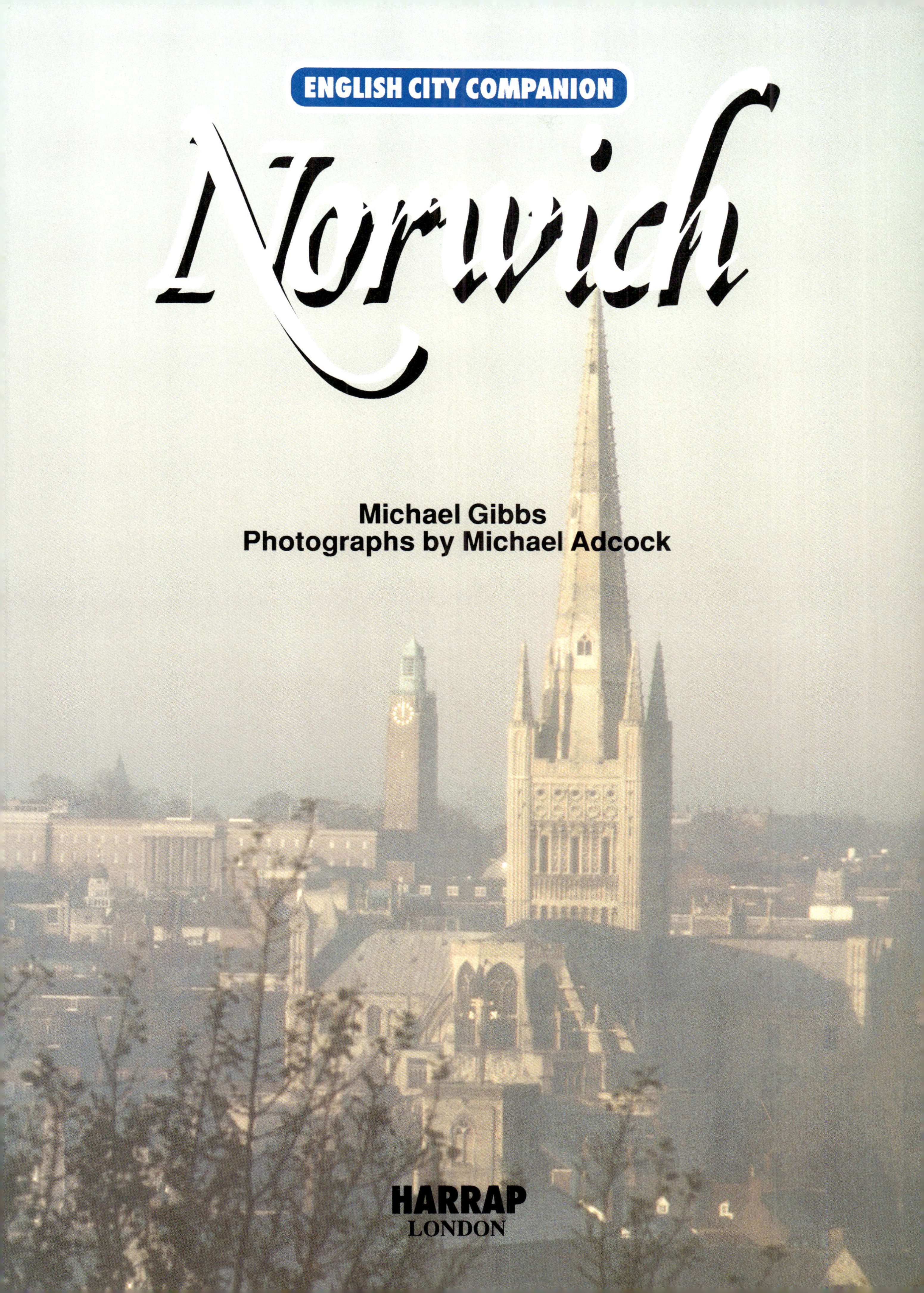

HARRAP
LONDON

First published in Great Britain 1991 by
Harrap Books Limited, Chelsea House,
26 Market Square, Bromley, Kent BR1 1NA

ISBN 0 245–60256–9

Designed by Roger King Graphic Studios, Poole.
Produced by Poole Typesetting (Wessex) Ltd.,
Bournemouth.
Printed and bound by Intellectual Publishing Co.,
Singapore.

~CONTENTS~

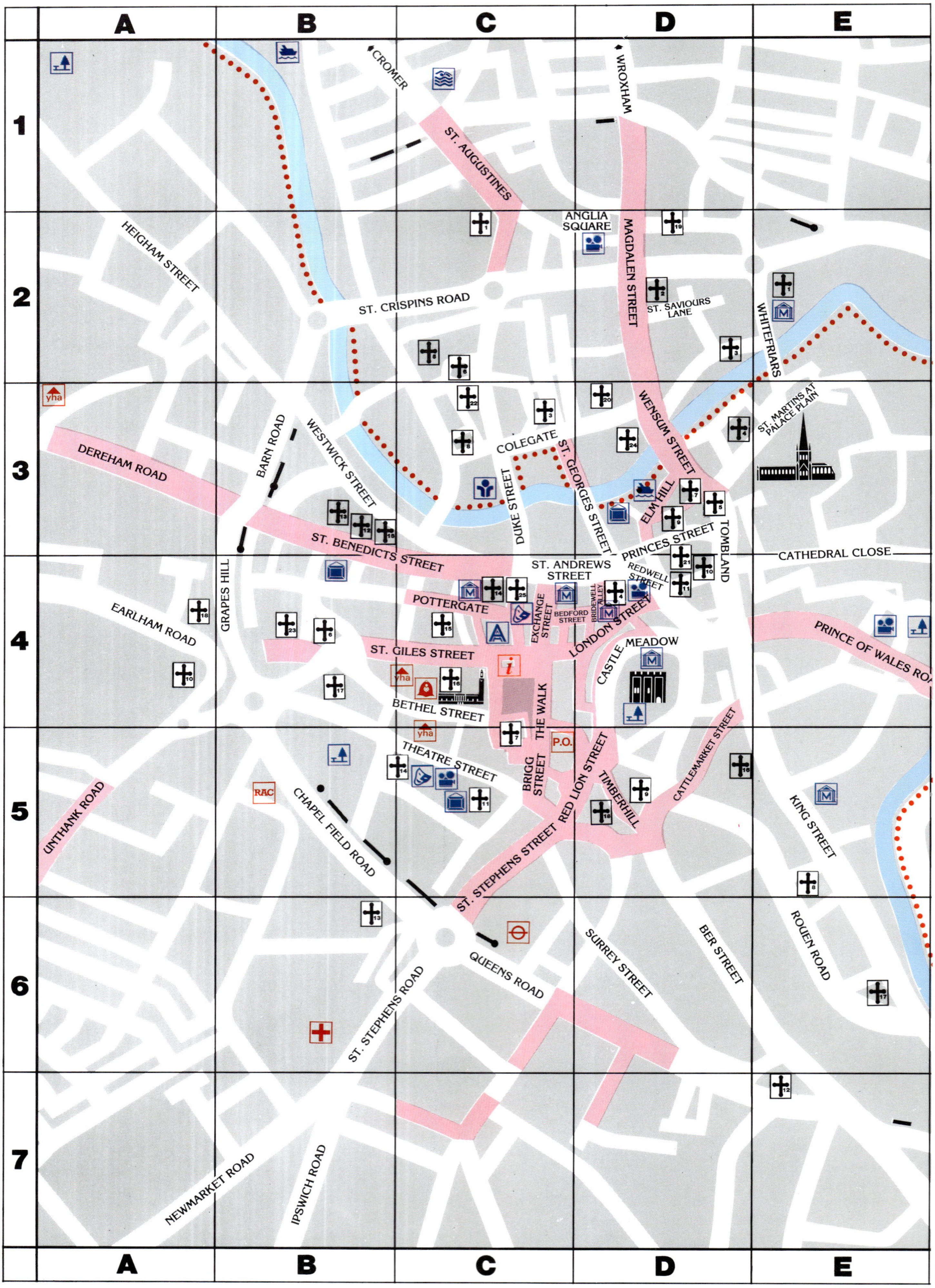
A
B
C
D
E
1
2
3
4
5
6
7
CROMER
WROXHAM
ST. AUGUSTINES
ANGLIA SQUARE
MAGDALEN STREET
HEIGHAM STREET
ST. CRISPINS ROAD
ST. SAVIOURS LANE
WHITEFRIARS
yha
WENSUM STREET
ST. MARTINS AT PALACE PLAIN
DEREHAM ROAD
BARN ROAD
WESTWICK STREET
COLEGATE
ST. GEORGES STREET
ELM HILL
DUKE STREET
PRINCES STREET
TOMBLAND
ST. BENEDICTS STREET
CATHEDRAL CLOSE
GRAPES HILL
ST. ANDREWS STREET
REDWELL STREET
EARLHAM ROAD
POTTERGATE
EXCHANGE STREET
BEDFORD STREET
BRIDEWELL ALLEY
LONDON STREET
CASTLE MEADOW
PRINCE OF WALES ROAD
ST. GILES STREET
BETHEL STREET
THE WALK
P.O.
THEATRE STREET
RAC
CHAPEL FIELD ROAD
BRIGG STREET
RED LION STREET
TIMBERHILL
CATTLEMARKET STREET
KING STREET
UNTHANK ROAD
ST. STEPHENS STREET
QUEENS ROAD
SURREY STREET
BER STREET
ROUEN ROAD
ST. STEPHENS ROAD
NEWMARKET ROAD
IPSWICH ROAD

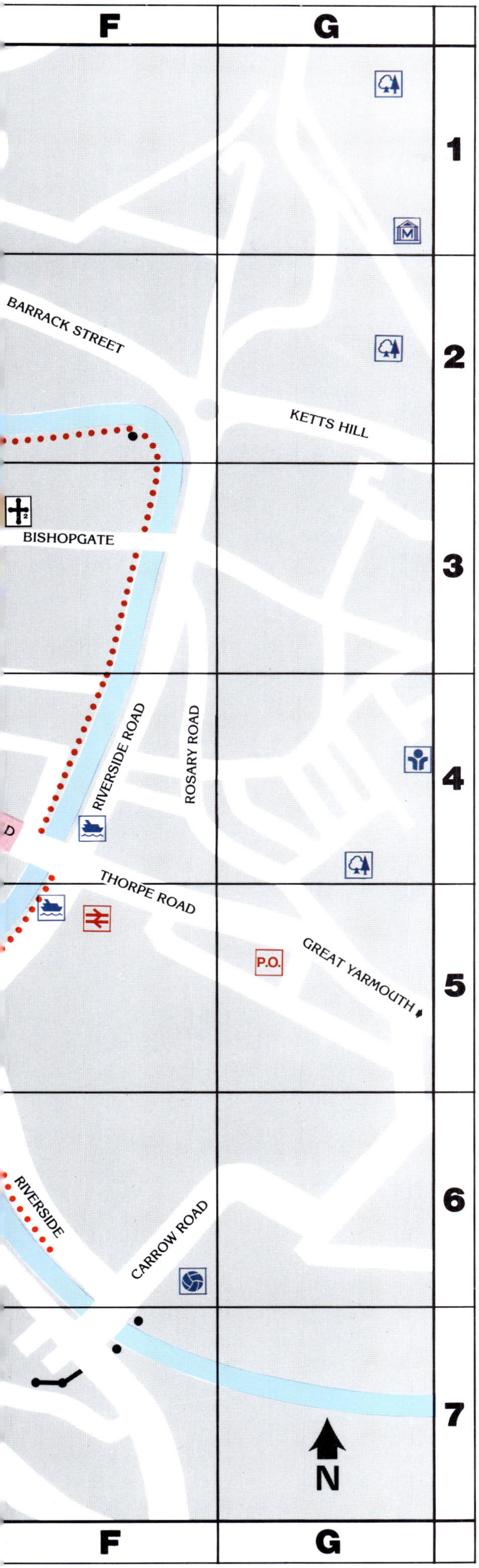

Norwich City Council

PLACES OF WORSHIP	GRID REFERENCE
4 St. Andrew	4D
1 St. Augustine	2C
3 St. George Colegate	3C
5 St. George Tombland	3D
6 St. Giles	4B
2 St. Helen	3F
10 St. John's Roman Catholic Cathedral	4A
12 St. John de Sepulchre	7E
9 St. John's Timberhill	5D
8 St. Julian	5E
7 St. Peter Mancroft	5C
11 St. Stephen	5C
22 Baptist	3C
23 Christadelphian	4B
25 Greek Orthodox	4C
13 Methodist	6B
14 Mosque	5C
24 Non Denominational	3D
15 Quakers	4C
16 Salvation Army	4C
17 Spiritualist	4B
18 Synagogue	4A
19 Undenominational	2D
20 Unitarian	3D
21 United Reformed	4D
Cathedral	3E

REDUNDANT CHURCHES	
18 All Saints – Day Centre	5D
3 St. Edmund – Vacant	2D
17 St. Etheledra – Arts Centre	6E
14 St. Gregory – Arts Centre	4C
1 St. James – Puppet Theatre, Tel: 629921	2E
15 St. Laurence – Vacant	3B
12 St. Margaret – Gymnasium	3B
5 St. Martin at Oak – Night Shelter	2C
4 St. Martin at Palace – Probation Day Centre	3D
6 St. Mary Coslany, – Craft Centre, Tel: 504794	2C
10 St. Mary the Less – Vacant	4D
11 St. Michael at Plea – Arts Centre	4D
8 St. Michael Coslany – Martial Arts Centre	3C
9 St. Peter Hungate – Museum	3D
16 St. Peter Parmentergate – Vacant	5D
2 St. Saviour – Badminton Hall	2D
7 St. Simon and St. Jude – Scout Shop	3D
13 St. Swithin – Norwich Arts Centre, Tel: 660352	3B

CITY WALLS	
Castle Museum	4D
City Hall	4C

MAIN SHOPPING STREETS

BUS STATION	
Eastern Counties – Surrey Street, Tel: 620491	6C

HOSPITAL	
Norfolk and Norwich – Brunswick Road, Tel: 628377	6B

HOSTELS	
YMCA – 48 St. Giles Street, Tel: 620269	4C
YWCA – 61 Bethel Street, Tel: 622059	5C
YHA – Turner Road, Tel: 627647	3A

MOTORING ORGANISATIONS	
RAC – 29 Chapelfield Road, Tel: 628255	5B

POLICE STATION	
Norwich City Police – Bethel Street, Tel: 621212	4C

POST OFFICE	GRID REFERENCE
Davey Place	5C
Main Sorting Office – Thorpe Road	5G

RIVERSIDE WALK

TOURIST INFORMATION CENTRE	
Guildhall – Gaol Hill, Tel: 666071	4C

TRAIN STATION	
British Rail – Thorpe Road, Tel: 632055	5F

BOAT HIRE	
Norwich Boat Hire – Riverside Road	4F
Rowing Boats – Wensum Park	1B
River bus pick up points – Elm Hill, Riverside Road	3D 5F

CINEMAS	
Cannon Cinema – Prince of Wales Road, Tel: 623312	4E
Cinema City – St. Andrews Hill, Tel: 622047	4D
Noverre Cinema – Theatre Street, Tel: 626402	5C
Odeon Cinema – Anglia Square, Tel: 621903	2D

FOOTBALL GROUND	
Norwich City Football Club – Carrow Road, Tel: 612131	7F

GALLERIES	
Advice Arcade Gallery – Guildhall Hill, Tel: 622233	4C
Assembly House – Theatre Street, Tel: 626402	5C
Contact Gallery – St. Benedicts, Tel: 760219	4B
Norwich School of Art – St. Georges Street, Tel: 610561	3D

MUSEUMS	
Bridewell Museum – Bridewell Alley, Tel: 667228	4D
Castle Museum – Castle Meadow, Tel: 611277	4D
Norfolk & Norwich Heritage Centre – Dragon Hall 123 King Street, Tel: 663922	5E
Royal Norfolk Regiment Museum – Britannia Barracks Britannia Road, Tel: 628455	1G
Strangers Hall Museum – Charing Cross, Tel: 667229	4C
Telephone Museum – St. Andrews Street Tel: 661714 (By appointment only)	4C
Jarrolds Printing Museum – Whitefriars Tel: 660211 (By appointment only)	2E

NATURAL AREAS	
Ketts Heights	2G
Mousehold Heath	1G
Rosary Cemetery	4G

PARKS AND GARDENS	
Anderson's Meadow – Mile Cross Road	1A
Castle Gardens – Castle Meadow	4D
Chapel Field Gardens – Chapel Field Road	5B
James Stuart Gardens – Recorder Road	4E

RECREATION CENTRES	
Crome Centre – Telegraph Lane East, Tel: 36697	4G
Duke Street Centre – Duke Street, Tel: 623469	3C

SWIMMING	
City of Norwich Baths – St. Augustines Street, Tel: 620164	1C

THEATRES	
Maddermarket Theatre – St. John's Alley	4C
Theatre Royal – Theatre Street	5C
Whiffler Theatre – Castle Gardens	4D

For information on other facilities outside of the central area, contact the Tourist Information Centre, Tel: 666071.

~INTRODUCTION~

When I first began training to become an official guide to Norwich, I was surprised that the mass of material I collected was not available in an easily readable and suitably indexed format.

Like all guides, I wrote up my material into notes on which I based the guided tours of the city that I undertook in the succeeding years. Finally, some seven years after qualifying as a guide, I stirred myself into action, determined to fulfil that original need, and began to rewrite the notes in the form of a comprehensive, alphabetical guide to the people, places and events which comprise the history of Norwich.

This book is the result. It represents, as far as I am aware, the first guide to the city of Norwich of this kind ever to be published. It is in no way intended to compete with the City Amenities Department's excellent Official Guide, but rather to complement it by concentrating in some detail on the major sights, events and personalities which the Official Guide can only, perforce, touch upon.

I hope that some at least of the three-quarters of a million people who visit Norwich each year will find that it adds to the pleasure they derive from the city and that it will also serve, perhaps, as a memento of their stay, to be dipped into at intervals after their departure.

I owe a debt of gratitude to many people, not least those who have, in the past, painstakingly researched and prepared material on aspects of the city and on whose writings I have freely drawn. The selected bibliography itemizes many of them, although I am conscious that many more remain anonymous, even to me.

Sincere thanks must go in particular to the City Planning Department for permission to reproduce their fine map; to Pam Petersen, and Trish Watson, of the Tourist Information Centre, for their unfailing encouragement; and to two of my fellow guides, Margaret Baker and Mike Adcock, for their thoroughness in checking the manuscript and making a number of pertinent and helpful suggestions, most of which have been incorporated. They also picked up many of my errors and these, too, have been corrected; having said that, any mistakes regarding facts, dates and interpretation that have crept into the text must be firmly down to me, not them.

Finally, it only remains to thank my own Margaret, who typed the manuscript, retyped it, altered it, corrected it and then worked into the small hours to amend it again, while gallantly battling to make sense of my appalling handwriting and eccentric typing – a labour of love indeed.

Michael Gibbs
Norwich
Autumn 1990

~KEY TO TEXT~

Indicates churches and other buildings which are normally open to the public.

(M) Indicates entries that are the subject of a green plaque or other memorial.

Entries in **bold type** are described in more detail under their own heading.

Words in *italics* are explained more fully in the glossary of terms.

~A~

ADAM & EVE

Thought to be the oldest pub in Norwich, the Adam & Eve had already seen the passage of three centuries when a battle between **Lord Sheffield's** troops and Kett's men raged outside during **Kett's Rebellion** on 1st August 1549.

It dates from at least 1249 and was probably established originally as a brewhouse for builders working on the **Cathedral** close by. During the 19th century it was much frequented by the men (and women) who sailed the Norfolk wherries. Indeed, a landlady who was a member of the Howes family, who leased the pub between 1845 and 1880, owned a wherry called the *Adam & Eve* which carried sea sand from Yarmouth to Norwich. The sand was used to fill the spittoons and cover the floors of the city's innumerable public houses (up to 900, according to the Norwich Gospel Temperance Union in 1892), including her own.

The pub was the favourite haunt of **James Blomefield Rush**, one of the most notorious Victorian murderers, who is believed to have planned the death of the Recorder of Norwich and his son while drinking there.

Despite many changes around it, the Adam and Eve has retained its ancient charm, characterized by the 16th-century flint and brick Dutch gable end with an unusual filled-in window at the top. The pub is owned by the **Great Hospital**, who lease it to the brewers.

AGRICULTURAL HALL

Built close to the original **cattle market**, and opened in 1882, this great barn of a building was designed by John Pearce, who embellished it with the stone carvings and columned pediments expected of him, while retaining an excellent classical line and proportion. Note the Prince of Wales plume carved in stone over the front entrance and the city arms on the pediment.

It was the venue for livestock shows, public meetings, fairs and circuses up until the last war, when the Army took it over. Afterwards it spent a decade as an extension of the Norwich sorting office. The council acquired the lease in 1957 and two years later it became Anglia House, headquarters of the regional television station, Anglia TV, who later linked it with the older **Hardwick House** next door.

Echoes of its original use still remain in the name Agricultural Hall Plain for the area where **Prince of Wales Road**, Bank Plain, **Castle Meadow** and Market Avenue meet in front of it.

ALL SAINTS

Flint-built like so many of the city's 31 pre-*Reformation* churches, All Saints dates from around 1320 and once stood in a densely populated area with its churchyard on the edge of the medieval swine market. It is an interesting mixture of ecclesiastical architecture; the windows in the *chancel* are in the *Decorated* style while those in the *nave*, aisle and tower have the flatter arches and vertical mullions of the 15th-century *Perpendicular* period. The square west tower is simple, short (prior to the belfry stage being re-built in 1913 it was even shorter) and unbuttressed. All Saints was made redundant in 1973 and is now a day centre for shoppers and visitors. It is entered by the south door, which is original and has admitted worshippers and visitors for more than 500 years.

ALL SAINTS GREEN

Scene of the ancient swine market, All Saints Green ran from the postern gate known as the **Brazen Doors** in the **city walls** to the south side of **All Saints** church. A densely populated area of the city up until the 1930s, when slum clearance began and many of the inhabitants were rehoused on the new Lakenham estates, it is worth a visit today for its Georgian buildings in various states of repair; the finest are the beautiful **St Catherine's Close** and the striking **Ivory House**, built in 1772 by **Thomas Ivory**, the most notable of Norwich's Georgian architects.

ALNWICK GATE

The least known but in many ways the prettiest of the four great gates in the walls which surround the **Cathedral**, the Alnwick takes its name from the Bishop of Norwich who began to build it but left it unfinished when he was transferred to Lincoln in 1436. (He also made a dreadful mess of the interior of the west end of the Cathedral, but that is another story....)

The large spaces of plain stonework over the smaller of the two doors, below the windows and around the central niche suggest that more decoration was intended. The fine carved doors were added by **Bishop Lyhart** while the battlements are a modern restoration. It is also known as the Bishop's Palace Gate, as it leads to both the **Bishop's Palace** and the modern **Bishop's House**.

ANCHOR BREWERY

Brewers prospered in 18th-century Norwich. There was good water available, filtered through chalk, and Norfolk grew some of the best malting barley in the world. In the early 1800s six major breweries dominated the trade with their own maltings and public houses. In 1801 Patteson's brewed 20,000 barrels of beer, more than many of the big London breweries – indeed, much of Norwich's beer was exported to the capital city. Bullards was one of the most important of the Norwich breweries. Part of their Anchor brewery – established in the 1840s although the building displays a stone with the date 1773 – can still be seen in Westwick Street, where it has been converted into an attractive complex of homes, shops, offices and restaurants.

All the great breweries gradually dissolved over the years into one conglomerate – and now, alas, even that is gone.

ST ANDREW

In few parts of Norwich are historical buildings so thick upon the ground as in St Andrew's Street. The church of St Andrew stands nearly opposite **St Andrew's and Blackfriars' Halls**, cheek by jowl with **Suckling House** and overlooking **Bridewell Alley**.

A 'live' church – not redundant like so many of its fellows and, therefore, open to the public – St Andrews is second in size only to **St Peter Mancroft**. The tower is the oldest part, dating from 1478. The rest of the church was rebuilt in 1506, making it a fine example of later *Gothic* architecture with huge windows and slender piers and arches. It is said that it was the ambition of the medieval mason to build a church entirely of glass and, with St Andrew, he began to come close to that ideal.

This was the great Whig church of the city and the Protestant sympathies of its parishioners can be gathered from the 16th-century inscriptions over the south door, which speak of a church 'lately translated from extreme idolatry' and of a Queen who 'set up the gospel and banished Popery'. The irony of this is in the fact that Bishop Underwood, pursuer and persecutor of the local heretics under Bloody Mary, lies buried in the centre aisle.

Don't miss the tomb of Sir John and Lady

Suckling in the chapel on the north side. Sir John lies beside his wife looking distinctly uncomfortable in his armour, propped up on his right elbow – as if he were about to tell her something – while their four children pray piously below.

Outside, at the east end, look for the sequence of 12 shields carved in stone. These are associated perhaps with William Appleyard, first Mayor of Norwich when the city received its Charter of Incorporation in 1404, or with his father Bartholomew, which would date them around 1380. From left to right, they are: the arms of the Holy Roman Empire; the arms of England; the arms of St Edmund; the arms of the city of Norwich (with an unusual version of the castle); the Royal arms of England from 1340 to 1405; the arms of St Andrew; a shield of the Crucifixion; a shield of the Blessed Sacrament; the arms of St George (or the Cathedral priory); the arms of **Bishop Henry Despenser**; the arms of Thomas Mowbray, who later became Duke of Norfolk; the final shield is unidentified but may represent the arms of a benefactor.

ST ANDREW'S AND BLACKFRIARS' HALLS

Home today of the Norwich Triennial Festival and scene of concerts, banquets, conferences, exhibitions, craft markets, book fairs and even flea markets, this great building was originally constructed as another of the city churches – the conventual church of the Dominican order of **Black Friars**. It has been described as the most complete remaining example in the country of a friars' church and one of the finest examples of *Perpendicular* architecture to be seen anywhere. At the *Reformation*, when the monastic orders were suppressed as part of Henry VIII's schism with the Catholic Church, the Black Friars' church and convent passed to the Crown, from whom the city – at the instigation of one of its greatest benefactors, **Augustine Steward** – bought them in 1540 as 'a fayre and large halle for the Mayor and his brethren for assemblyes' and as a school, granary and civic chapel.

The King agreed £81 as the price but later decided this was not enough (or suffered one of his periodic cash crises), for the city chamberlains had to pay a further £152 for the lead on the roof, which had in fact been specified in the original purchase price. Nevertheless, for a total cost of £233, Augustine Steward secured a bargain for the city, and the old church has since been used as an assembly room, municipal chapel, cloth hall, granary, corn exchange, workhouse, artillery ground – even, during **Kett's Rebellion**, as a stable for the horses of the Earl of Warwick.

The Black Friars moved to this site and built their first church here between 1326 and 1413, when a fire destroyed a large part of the building. It is likely that the present church was constructed on the remains of the first; certainly six windows on the south side of the *nave* and the great east window of the *chancel* survive from the earlier building.

The fine *clerestory* windows on the south side are flanked by the arms of the Erpingham family and were probably financed by Friar Robert Erpingham, Rector of Bracon Ash, in memory of his father, **Sir Thomas Erpingham**, the hero of Agincourt. The beams for both the *hammerbeam* roof in the *nave* and the roof of the *chancel* were the gift of another famous Norwich family, the **Pastons** who lived nearby in **Elm Hill** (they were also partially responsible for the reconstruction of **St Peter Hungate**).

Today the nave of the church forms St Andrew's Hall, the chancel is Blackfriars' Hall (look for Beechey's magnificent portrait of **Horatio Nelson**) and the friars' preaching yard forms the car park. Of the original convent, the cloisters and the remains of the 13th-century Becket chapel have been restored (the latter with a particularly garish roof) and you can enjoy a cup of coffee in the crypt, which contains some of the oldest work on the site, dating from 1258 when the **Sack Friars** were in residence.

ANGUISH, THOMAS (1538–1617)

Mayor of Norwich in 1611, he is best remembered for two events – one tragic, the other philanthropic.

The first occurred during his mayoralty. At a civic reception in front of his house in the parish of St George Tombland (where the entrance to the **Maid's Head Hotel** stands today), there was panic in the crowd when the fireworks exploded prematurely and 33 people were trampled to death. All were buried at the nearby church of **St Simon and St Jude**. Thereafter the city council banned fireworks on feast and guild days.

The second came about after his death, for in his will he endowed a hospital for children in **Fishergate** to be used not in the medical sense but for 'the keepinge, bringinge up and teachinge, of younge and very poore children, borne, and brought up in this City of Norwich, and especially for suche as for wante lye in the Streets, Vaughtes, Doores, and Windowes, whereby many of them fall into greate and grievous diseases and lameness, as they are fit for no Profession ever after.' His Bluecoat School, as it came to be known, was the first to provide education for the poor and destitute of Norwich. And very picturesque they must have looked, with the boys dressed in red muffin caps, blue sparrow-tailed coats and striped waistcoats and the girls in poke bonnets, blue gowns and cross-over kerchiefs. The pupils were taught to read and write; the girls also learned house-craft and the boys were bound as apprentices as soon as they were old enough. The boys' school closed in the mid-1800s but the girls' school continued until as recently as 1941.

Using the investments and endowments of lands, the Anguish Foundation continues as an educational charity, especially concerned with the sons and daughters of Freemen of Norwich. Thomas Anguish is buried in **St George Tombland** and a memorial to him may still be seen, although somewhat obscured by the organ.

ANNE OF BOHEMIA (1366–1394)

Daughter of the Holy Roman Emperor Charles IV, and Queen of England at 17, Anne visited Norwich with her 16-year-old husband, Richard II, in 1383. The King and Queen came to the city as part of their progress around the country, visiting areas which had been particularly diligent in suppressing the **Peasants' Revolt** in 1381.

The Queen must have caused a sensation in **Holm-strete** (now **Bishopgate**) by riding her horse side-saddle – something the people had not seen before, as she introduced this style into the country – on her way to view the progress that was being made in rebuilding the church of **St Helen**. To commemorate the visit, the Bishop of Norwich, **Henry Despenser**, had the 252 panels in the wooden roof of the church painted with the double-headed eagle, the symbol of the Holy Roman Empire. These panels are still a feature of the church and the **Great Hospital**, with which it is closely associated.

Anne's brother, the King of Bohemia, was called Wenceslas – so next time you sing of a king of that name, looking out on the feast of St Stephen, think of young Anne, new bride of a King of England and destined to die before she was 30, riding side-saddle in Norwich's medieval streets, to the delight and astonishment of the populace.

ARCADE, ROYAL

Norwich's pre-eminent Victorian and Edwardian architect, **George Skipper**, was in a fanciful mood when he planned this shopping arcade, built in 1899, as a magnificent example of Art Nouveau. Running from **Gentleman's Walk** to **Back of the Inns**, its combination of tiles and tracery is irresistible. The architectural historian, Sir Nikolaus Pevsner, described it as 'innocent in front but very naughty when its back is turned'. Joseph Stannard designed the 'innocent' front while Skipper was responsible for the naughty bits.

Above: All Saints Church, Westlegate.

Above right: St Andrew's Church by night.

Below: Blackfriars cloisters.

Below right: Interior, Royal Arcade.

The site used to be occupied by the **Royal Hotel**, which was rebuilt at Agricultural Hall Plain in 1897.

ARMADA HOUSE

This late-16th century, timber-framed, two-storey house – possibly a reconstruction of a 15th-century dwelling – is officially known as Garsett House after an early resident, Robert Garsett, who died in 1613 and is commemorated in the Suckling Chapel of **St Andrew's Church** across the road. It became known as Armada House in Victorian times in the belief that the house timbers were salvaged from one of the Spanish galleons forming part of the ill-fated Armada which set out to conquer England in 1588 and was comprehensively defeated in the Channel. The fleet was blown around the British Isles in a great gale and a number of galleons were known to have been wrecked off the east coast, so the story may well be true. Certainly the date 1589 – the year after the defeat of the Armada – is carved into the cornice at first-floor height on the left-hand side of the building.

Two other items of particular interest can be seen. High up on the front of the house is an original circular firemark of Phoenix Insurance, a reminder of the days when insurance companies organized fire brigades and firemarks identified insured properties, before street numbering was introduced around 1840. On the south side – which is curiously truncated as a result of the arrival in 1900 of the **tramway system** and the need for a road to be cut through from **St Andrew Street** to Redwell Street – is what remains of an insulated fixture which held up the overhead wires for the trams. It is one of only six to be found in the city.

ASSEMBLY HOUSE

'Seen through its superb wrought-iron gates, placed there in 1902, it is like an 18th-century town house that has somehow escaped the sweeping demolitions of the post-war periods.' This is how Norwich historian Geoffrey Goreham describes the Assembly House, one of the finest creations of **Thomas Ivory**, who built it in 1754 on the site of the medieval college of **St Mary-in-the-Fields** and between the two wings of a 17th-century house which are still standing (the right-hand wing is the **Noverre Cinema**).

For over a century the Assembly House was a meeting place for the fashionable few – in what was the music room 400 guests danced the minuet to celebrate the victory won (at the cost of **Nelson's** life) at Trafalgar (1805).

It served for 60 years as the Norwich High School for Girls (**Edith Cavell** was one of its pupils) and was used by the Army during the Second World War as a centre for teaching camouflage techniques. The Norwich shoe manufacturer, Henry Sexton, bought the building and restored it to its original 18th-century glory at a cost of £70,000 in 1950 and gave it to the city with the wish that 'it should be dedicated to the use and enjoyment of the whole community'. Today that wish is fulfilled for it is used for meetings, exhibitions, displays and concerts and has an excellent restaurant where a meal or a drink can be taken in surroundings which recall a more gracious and (for a privileged minority) a more leisured era.

ST AUGUSTINE

Standing close to where **St Augustine's Gate** gave access to the city from the north-west, this unusually proportioned church – the *chancel* is as long as the *nave*, while the nave is as wide as it is long – is the only one in Norwich to have its tower constructed from brick rather than traditional flint. The tower was rebuilt in 1687, to replace one that had fallen some 10 years earlier, and its colour led to the worshippers being known as the 'red steeplers'. The church was much restored, inside and out, late in the last century, when a new south porch was added. Several of the

Decorated-style windows in the nave and chancel date from this period although the *Perpendicular clerestory* windows are believed to be original. A reminder that the weaving trade once provided the main means of support for inhabitants of this part of the city can be found in a tablet on the south aisle wall. It was erected in memory of Thomas Clabburn, who died in 1858, by 600 of his weavers – most of whom, it must be said, would have worked from their own homes.

ST AUGUSTINE'S GATE

See **Gates.**

AUSTIN FRIARS

Followers of St Augustine and the third of the friary orders to establish themselves in Norwich, they inhabited a priory between **King Street** and the river of which nothing now remains. The priory was built between 1360 and 1368, and incorporated the late 13th-century church of St Michael. Henry Howard, 6th Duke of Norfolk, built **Howard House** – which still stands – on the site in the late 17th century. See also *Friaries*.

B

BACK OF THE INNS

Before the arrival of the railways drove them out of business, stage-coaches provided the only reliable – if uncomfortable – means of transport for covering long distances. The starting and finishing points, and the staging posts in between, were the inns of England, and in Norwich most of the great inns were to be found in **Gentleman's Walk** – the Half Moon, the King's Head, the Bear, the Royal, the Star, the Castle and the **Bell** – standing in a half-crescent between **London Street** and Orford Hill. The road behind them was, and still is, called Back of the Inns and it was here, at the beginning of each day, that the detritus of innumerable teams of horses would be swept from the inn yards. Definitely a place not to put your foot in it.

(M)

BACON HOUSE

Built by a wealthy merchant, Henry Bacon, who was sheriff in 1548 and mayor in 1557 and 1566, Bacon House was used for many purposes over the centuries – pawnbrokers, college, shoe works, tobacco factory, café, theatre – before the city council saved it from destruction by taking over the lease and investing £83,000 in renovating it in the mid-1970s. Today it is a fine example in flint and timber of a Tudor businessman's property, used as the premises for a club and various small businesses.

You can still see Henry Bacon's initials and merchant's mark in the *spandrels* of the main doorway and over the central window. The other door has had a somewhat peripatetic history. Dated 1596, it was originally in a house in Bedford Street, from where it was removed to Carrow Abbey in 1886 and from there to its present location.

As a prominent citizen, Bacon entertained the **Earl of Warwick** when he arrived in the city in 1549 to put down **Kett's Rebellion** but he made himself unpopular with many of Kett's supporters in the city by displaying prominently outside his house the Earl's badge of the bear and ragged staff.

Above: Armada House.

Below: Exterior, Royal Arcade.

Above: Bacon House.

Above: St Benedict's Tower.

Below: Bell Hotel.

BANK OF ENGLAND COURT

In the days when the Bank of England had premises in places other than Threadneedle Street (as the Bank of Scotland has many branches south of the border today), the Norwich branch stood in this old court for 24 years. It is a pleasant surprise to find, leading off narrow and busy Queen Street, this quiet and spacious oasis with its graceful 18th-century buildings and three massive Georgian doorways, one of which is said originally to have been a façade, opening on to a brick wall. Even more of a surprise awaits the visitors who take the passage through to the residential development behind, for here they will find the 'hidden' church of **St Mary the Less**.

Old Bank of England Court was the scene of an unusual wager in 1810 when a noted local horseman, Sir Lambert Blackwell of Easton, accepted a challenge to drive a coach and four horses into the court, turn it round and drive out again...without touching the walls. No mean judge of distance (not to say horses), he duly won the bet.

BARKING DICKY

One of only five original thatched properties left in Norwich – the others are **Pykerell's House**, a dwelling in **Hampshire Hog Yard**, the **Briton's Arms** and the **Hermitage** in Bishopgate – this 16th-century building standing next to **All Saints Church** is now the home of a finance company. With the church, it is the only original building remaining in **Westlegate** – both, unfortunately, are overshadowed by the hideous modern tower of Westlegate House.

The property takes its curious name from the time when it was a public house called the Light Horseman. The pub sign was said to be so badly painted that the horse in question looked like a cross between a dog and a donkey – or, in Norfolk parlance, a 'dicky'.

BASSINGHAM GATEWAY

No, not one of the old city gates, but a splendid stone doorway set in the south-west corner of the **Guildhall**. It was placed there in 1857 from the home of a Tudor goldsmith named John Bassingham which stood between 57 and 59 London Street. It bears the arms of Henry VIII, the city of Norwich and the Goldsmiths Company.

BELL HOTEL

This ancient building was one of the city's principal coaching inns, with a coachway (now filled in) running from front to back. The original bell was sounded at midday to indicate to farmers attending the nearby **cattle market** that it was time for dinner (preferably at the Bell). It probably took its name from the bell foundry which was discovered recently in Timberhill.

ST BENEDICT

Before the Luftwaffe's bombs swept much of the parish out of existence in 1942, this must have been an attractive little church with a round tower, a single north aisle, north and south porches and an aisle arcade supported, unusually, on cast-iron columns. All that remains now, between **St Benedict Street** and **Pottergate**, is the tower. The lower round portion is believed to be *Norman* and the octagonal upper storey – a feature of several East Anglian round towers – probably dates from the 15th century.

ST BENEDICT'S GATE

See **Gates.**

ST BENEDICT'S STREET

A pleasant thoroughfare of mostly 18th and 19th century buildings and some good shops situated between **Charing Cross** and Dereham Road, chiefly remarkable for its profusion of medieval churches standing within a few yards of one another – **St Gregory, St Laurence, St Margaret, St Swithin** and **St Benedict** – all now redundant.

BER STREET

Known for many years as 'Blood and guts street' from the large number of butchers' shops and slaughterhouses which abounded in close proximity to the old **cattle market**, this is one of the city's oldest roads, leading to the ancient and now vanished settlement of **Needham**. Originally it was known as Burgh Street. It was a street with an unsavoury reputation, of dark yards and narrow alleys, and pubs by the dozen, much frequented by the drovers who brought their beasts to market. It traverses the edge of a plateau which drops sharply down to the east towards the **River Wensum**.

The remnants of **Ber Street Gate**, set in a pleasant little rose garden by Foulger's Opening at the Bracondale end of the street, are the only physical remains of any of the 12 **gates** which once gave entry to the city.

Nearby, on the corner of **Finkelgate**, is the church of **St John de Sepulchre** with its great tower which has been a city landmark for centuries. Half-way along are the ruins of St Bartholomew's Church, which was desecrated as long ago as 1549 and gradually fell into decay, but not before doing duty as a tallow factory and a cattle shed. At the end, by Thorn Lane, only a plaque marks the site of **St Michael at Thorn**, which pre-dated the *Conquest*, and where many of those who died or were executed at the **Castle** found a final resting place. The church was one of six lost to enemy action in 1942. The spot is now occupied by **Prospect House**, the head office of Eastern Counties Newspapers.

BER STREET GATE

See **Gates.**

(M)

BETHEL HOSPITAL

Built in 1713 by Mary Chapman, the widow of the Revd. Samuel Chapman, this is the oldest psychiatric hospital in Britain still being used for its original purpose. Both Mary Chapman and her husband had relations who were mentally ill and Samuel left money in his will to establish an institution 'for the habitation of poor lunaticks, and not for natural-born fools and idiots' (presumably then, as now, it was often difficult to tell the difference). From the start Mary showed a progressive attitude towards her patients, with medical supervision and facilities for recreation and worship. This was remarkable in the early part of a century in which it was more normal to lock the afflicted away and then charge the public for the pleasure of coming to laugh at them. Mary Chapman died in 1724 but her hospital continued to pioneer new methods of curing mental illness. Today, more than 275 years after its foundation, and looking much the same as Mary knew it, the Bethel Hospital is used to treat children and adolescents with psychiatric problems.

(M)

BILNEY, THOMAS (1495 – 1531)

Protestant preacher burned at the stake in the **Lollards Pit** in 1531 for heresy. Prior to his execution, he was imprisoned in the crypt of the **Guildhall**. It was here, according to Foxe's 'Book of Martyrs' published in 1596, that he held his hand in the flame of a candle to try his courage for the terrible death that awaited him. His 'crime' was to preach against superstition and abuses in the Church.

(M)

BISHOP BRIDGE

Believed to be the oldest bridge in England still in daily use by traffic, this ancient span dates from 1340. It stands at the point where one of Norfolk's oldest roads entered the city from the east, probably used by the Romans before there was a city at all; they would have crossed the **River Wensum** by a ford at this point.

It was the only bridge giving access to the city from outside (all the others were within the city walls) and, as it formed part of the city's defences, a fortified gatehouse was erected at its western end.

The bridge was the scene of bitter fighting during **Kett's Rebellion**. It was also the route taken by men and women on their way to the stake at **Lollards Pit** to die for their beliefs in the 15th and 16th centuries.

BISHOP GATE

In modern parlance, this is the road which leads from **Bishop's Bridge** to **St Martin at Palace** Plain; it was called **Holm-strete** in medieval times. Up until the end of the 18th century, however, Bishop Gate was the name of the 14th–century fortified gatehouse on the western side of **Bishop Bridge** – one of the 12 gates to the city. It was a substantial and handsome gate with an unusual large double window above the arch. In 1790 there were complaints that, the opening between the turrets being only nine feet wide, 'large loads of hay were so wedged as to their destruction' – an interesting early example of a Norwich traffic jam. There were also fears that the gatehouse was too heavy for the bridge to bear and in 1791 it was demolished at a cost of £170. The only reminder of this great edifice is to be found in the semi-circular projections on either side of the bridge parapet where the base of the turrets stood.

BISHOP'S HOUSE

The modern home of the Bishop of Norwich, built in 1959 and situated just inside the **Alnwick Gate**.

BISHOP'S PALACE

The predecessor of the **Bishop's House**, built originally to the north of the **Cathedral** by **Herbert de Losinga** and much restored in the 1850s. It has within its structure, however, considerable remains from the *Norman* and medieval periods, including a Norman kitchen and a 15th-century roof installed by **Bishop Walter Lyhart**, who was responsible for the stone vaulting in the nave of the Cathedral. The gates to the palace situated at the north-west corner of the Cathedral were brought here from the **Octagon Chapel** in **Colegate**. Since 1960, the palace has been part of the **Norwich School**.

BISHOP'S PALACE GATE

See **Alnwick Gate**.

(M)

BLACK FRIARS

Established in southern Europe by St Dominic in 1218 as the Order of Friars Preachers – known as Black Friars from the colour of their robes – they reached England in 1221 and Norwich five years later. Their first home in the city was the church of St John the Baptist in the **Colegate** area but it lacked access to river transport and, in 1307, they applied to take over the priory of the suppressed **Sack Friars** near **Elm Hill**, on which they established their great conventual church which still stands as **St Andrew's and Blackfriars' Halls**. See also **Friaries**.

(M)

BLACKFRIARS BRIDGE

A link between this attractive little bridge and the Bank of England might seem unlikely – but it exists. There was a bridge across the **Wensum** at this point in the 14th century, rebuilt in 1483. The present bridge was designed in 1783 by **Sir John Soane**, a Norwich-based architect. He was also responsible for the gaol at the **Castle** (built between 1789

Above: Bishop Bridge.

Right: Black Tower and city walls.

and 1793) before taking himself into the big league by becoming architect to the Bank of England. The cast iron railings were added around 1820. Also known as St George's Bridge, it is the oldest bridge within the old city precincts.

BLACKFRIARS' HALL

See **St Andrew's and Blackfriars' Hall.**

BLACK TOWER

The longest remaining stretch of the **city walls** is a section of around 160ft running up Carrow Hill to the Black Tower, which was the largest of all the towers in the walls and the only one to survive in its entirety (the **Cow Tower** stands on its own and, although used defensively, was never a part of the wall). Also known as Boteler's or the Governor's or Commander's tower, it was used during the plague of 1665/66 as a pest-house where victims of the plague were isolated. It has also been a prison, a snuff mill, and a cotton spinning mill. Carrow Hill is a comparatively new name, having been built in 1817 to provide work for the unemployed. An earlier name for this spot was Butter Hills.

SIR LAMBERT BLACKWELL

See **Bank of England Court.**

BLOMEFIELD, FRANCIS (1705–1751)

Anybody writing the history of Norwich and Norfolk owes an incalculable debt to Blomefield, who completed two volumes of the 'History of Norfolk' and was engaged upon a third when he contracted smallpox on a visit to London and died at the age of 46. Educated at Gonville and Caius College, Cambridge, which has many links with Norwich, he started the first volume in 1733 when Rector of Fersfield, near Diss. It was a great success and reprinted twice, but it failed to make its author much money. He decided to move to Norwich to write the next volume and obtained a curacy at **St George Tombland**. It is difficult to understand how he found time to look after the parish as he persevered with Volume II in a house which still exists, in **Willow Lane**.

Although he left behind a record of many buildings and documents which have since disappeared, Francis Blomefield's greatest success was to find in the archive room at Oxnead – the Norfolk country house built by William Paston – the correspondence of the **Paston** family. The Paston letters have achieved a fame of their own and, although edited by others, it was through Blomefield that they were discovered.

BLOWE, GREAT

Although Norwich was a Parliamentary city during the Civil War – Cromwell raised his famous Maiden Troop here – there was always some sympathy for the Royal cause, which was how the Great Blowe of 1648 came about.

A large house in Bethel Street was in use as the headquarters of the Roundhead County Committee. A rumour went round the city that the Mayor, who was a Royalist, was about to be arrested on a charge of sedition. A mob quickly formed to prevent the arrest and decided to arm itself from the arsenal of weapons contained in the committee house. In the excitement of 'liberating' guns and gunpowder, caution was thrown to the winds. Lighted lanterns were taken into the cellars to look for more arms. One man was seen entering the house with his pipe well alight! The result was inevitable – up went some 96 barrels of gunpowder. Around 100 people were killed or badly injured, **St Peter Mancroft** and **St Stephen's** lost a lot of stained glass and the house disappeared altogether. (**Mary**

Chapman was to build her **Bethel Hospital** on this same site some 65 years later).

Erasmus Earl, M.P. for Norwich in the Long Parliament and Sergeant-at-Law under Cromwell, passed Christmas Day sentencing to death those ringleaders who survived the explosion.

BOOM TOWERS

Part of the original defences, the towers on either side of the river near **Carrow Bridge** were built in 1334 to control vessels approaching the city and to collect tolls. A double chain of iron was slung between the towers and raised and lowered by a windlass. Though now in ruins, the towers can still be seen. In the late 18th century the cylindrical shape of the tower just below the Carrow bridge-keeper's lodge was found to be just the right shape for a coke oven; the coke was then used in nearby maltings to roast barley for brewing.

(M)

BORROW, GEORGE (1803–1881)

Writer, wanderer, linguist and friend to the Romanies, George Borrow lived in a house at the junction of **Willow Lane** and **Cow Hill**. A popular author in his day, his titles included *Romany Rye*, *Lavengro* and *The Bible in Spain*. He is credited with the phrase 'Norwich a fine old city ... view it from what side you will'. His house is now tucked away behind a new development.

BRAZEN DOORS

Also known as the Iron Door, this was the gate which gave access to All Saints Green from south-west of the city. It was a plain, square gatehouse with battlements and, presumably, a door cast from metal. Like all the city gates, it was demolished in the late 18th century.

BRIDEWELL ALLEY

One of the oldest shopping streets in the city, Bridewell Alley offers a delightful view of a typically bustling narrow, crowded Norwich lane as it must have looked in medieval times. Indeed, many local people feel it to be superior to Elm Hill in its atmosphere, appearance and – above all – sense of life. Lying between St Andrew's Street and Bedford Street, and buttressed at one end by the fine flint tower of **St Andrew's Church**, the alley has much to admire, including the **Bridewell Museum** with its superb knapped flint wall, Colman's loving reconstruction of a **mustard shop** and Hovell's basket shop, which has twice been saved from fire in recent years. A large fish over a former tackle shop reminds us of the days when much of the population of the city was illiterate; weavers' windows, designed to admit as much light as possible and among the last examples in Norwich, can also be seen. The deep doorways of the shops indicate the existence of jettied, timber-framed houses above. Don't miss it.

(M)

BRIDEWELL MUSEUM

Situated in a medieval merchant's house, built in 1325 and associated with the father of William Appleyard, first Mayor of Norwich in 1404, the Bridewell has been a museum of local industries and rural crafts since 1925.

It takes its name from the use of the building in the late 16th century as a Bridewell prison/workhouse (the name is based upon the first such reform home near St Bride's Well in London). People found begging or wandering in the streets were committed here and made to work from 5 a.m. until 8 p.m. with only a 45-minute break – 30 minutes for food and 15 minutes for prayer.

An inscription at the entrance tells us that the wall which runs between **Bridewell Alley** and St Andrews Hill, and which forms the north wall of the Bridewell, is 'esteemed to be the finest piece of flintwork in England'. And

Left: Sir Thomas Browne's statue and St Peter Mancroft.

Below: Carnary Chapel and Erpingham Gate.

Above: The Castle in springtime.

Below: The Castle and Davey Place.

so it is ... a dramatic black sweep of wall beautifully constructed by long dead craftsmen with forgotten skills, from squared flints, each joint a perfect mortarless fit. In some cases slight gaps between the knapped flints have been packed with tiny flint fragments, said to be an aid to making a flint wall damp- and frost-proof – an important point when the premises were used by a merchant to store his goods in an undercroft while he and his family lived over the top. The flint chips are known as gallets and the whole process as galletting.

BRIDGE HOUSE

7Not many of the green plaques marking places of special interest in Norwich are wrongly situated but one on the Bridge House almost certainly is. It describes this ancient pub as being the site of the **Lollards Pit** but an earlier and more reliable marker – now vanished – erected by the Protestant Alliance in 1931 places it some way to the right, on the site of what is now the car park of a DIY store. Taking its name from Bishop Bridge, which stands opposite, the Bridge House was the only building on the east side of the river until the great upsurge in house-building outside the city initiated by the early Victorians.

BRIDGE, REVD WILLIAM (1600–1670)

Rector of **St Peter Hungate**, he was expelled from the established church in 1636 for preaching Puritanism at **St George Tombland** and fled to Holland to become minister of the English Church there. He founded the Independants, who became the Congregationalists, who in turn built in 1693 the first and oldest of Norwich's non-conformist chapels, the **Old Meeting House**. It contains a memorial to him.

BRITON'S ARMS

The only building in Elm Hill to survive the disastrous fire of 1507, this lovely old coffee house (one of only five thatched buildings remaining in the city) is a delight with its pastel colouring, projecting floors, mullioned windows and arched doorway at the back. The oldest part dates from the 14th century when it was known as Le Godes Hous. Over the centuries it has been the home of 'barbours' or surgeons, and used for weaving, cordwaining, and saddle-making. It was even a nunnery, or more specifically a beguinage, where a small group of women lived as a religious community without taking formal vows. Beguinages were very popular in Holland but Norwich is the only English city known to have contained one.

It became an alehouse in 1760, known as the King's Arms, but 40 years later this was changed to the Briton's Arms when a wave of revolutionary fervour swept the city. When it was de-licensed in the late 1950s, the brewery presented the building to the city.

BROWNE, SIR THOMAS (1605–1682)

'A very distinguished man, Sir Thomas Browne, Kt. Doctor of Medicine, aged 77, who died on 19th October, 1682, sleeps in this coffin of lead. By the dust of his alchemic body he transmutes it into a coffer of gold. RIP.'

Sir Thomas would have approved of this epitaph, inscribed in Latin on his coffin in a vault in **St Peter Mancroft**, his parish church.

He is one of the city's most famous sons – a renowned philosopher, writer, naturalist, antiquarian and moralist, and the only person to be honoured within the city by two green plaques and a statue! The plaques mark the site of his home in Orford Place and a meadow he leased just off the **Lower Close** of the **Cathedral**. The statue is set in **Hay Hill** and depicts him examining a burial urn, a subject on which he wrote a definitive book. Although identified so strongly with Norwich, Sir Thomas was born in London and settled in the city at the age of 32 after qualifying as a doctor.

His first book, *Religio Medici*, brought him

great fame at home and abroad and he went on to make his name in a number of other fields, notably natural history; he established a collection of plants, birds and animals which the diarist Evelyn described as 'a cabinet of rarities'.

He was knighted by King Charles II in a splendid ceremony in **St Andrew's Hall** in September 1671. Yet, despite all his learning and clarity of thought, he was still tied to the superstitions and savagery of his age. Asked to examine two women accused of casting spells on children at Lowestoft, causing them to 'vomit crooked pins and broad-headed tu-penny nails', he said that he was clearly of the opinion 'that the persons were bewitched and that the Devil in such cases did work upon the bodies of men and women'. The two women, who were on the verge of being acquitted until Sir Thomas's intervention, were condemned and hanged.

There is a curious and gruesome footnote to the history of Sir Thomas. While another grave was being prepared in the *chancel* of St Peter Mancroft, his coffin was accidentally damaged and the skull removed by a sexton. He sold it to a Doctor Lubbock who eventually gave it to the **Norfolk and Norwich Hospital**. After an unseemly quarrel between the hospital and the church over the cost of re-interment, it was not until 1922 that the skull was reunited with the rest of the remains and Sir Thomas (or rather his head) was given the unusual privilege of a second funeral service, 240 years after the first.

Collectors of curious historical facts may also like to know that Sir Thomas was born on 19th October, died on 19th October, and his statue on Hay Hill was unveiled on the same date.

C

(M)

CAIUS, JOHN (1510–1573)

Born in the parish of **St Etheldreda, King Street**, he became physician to three monarchs – the boy King Edward VI, Mary Tudor and Elizabeth I – while never deviating from his Catholic beliefs. He became a wealthy man and used his riches to refound his old Cambridge college, Gonville Hall, in 1557. He became Master of the college but his strict Catholic views put him on a collision course with the Protestant fellows and he was forced to resign. The college is now called Gonville and Caius and many Norfolk men have gone there, several of them becoming Masters. Senior members of the University of East Anglia, which is situated just outside the city, have dining and other privileges there.

CARMELITE FRIARS

See **White Friars.**

(M)

CARNARY CHAPEL

Life in medieval Norwich was, for most of its citizens, hard, brutal and short. And, when it was over, matters didn't improve much; the average corpse was wrapped in a woollen shroud (coffins were only for the rich) and interred in a shallow grave, from which it was likely to reappear, in skeletal form, a few years later. The Carnary College, comprising four priests, was established by Bishop Salmon in 1316 and the *Decorated* chapel in the **Upper Close**, known as Bishop Salmon's Chantry, was built to accommodate bones 'clean of flesh' from the overloaded burial grounds of

Above: East end of Cathedral.

Left: Cathedral spire by night.

Below: Cathedral from Upper Close.

the city. Bones were regarded as sacred – they held the soul, it was believed – and they were placed in the undercroft of the chapel, while the priests said Masses for the souls of the departed.

After the *Reformation*, the building was acquired by the city to house the **Norwich School**. It still belongs to the school, which restored the chapel in 1940.

CARROW BRIDGE

The second structure to span the **Wensum** at Carrow, this counter-balanced lift bridge was opened by the Prince of Wales (later the Duke of Windsor) on 27th July, 1923. The work of the city engineer, Mr A. E. Collins, it is officially a single-leaf, roller bascule-type bridge, which takes 3½ minutes to raise and a minute to lower as it temporarily interrupts traffic using Carrow Road to admit large vessels to the **Port of Norwich**. There was no crossing at Carrow until 1810, when the original toll bridge was built 200 yards downstream of the present bridge.

CARROW PRIORY

This Benedictine nunnery was established in the 12th century and situated outside the city walls, close to the **Conesford Gate**. The community exchanged wool and corn with the city, particularly at Carrow Fair. **Julian of Norwich** is believed to have been educated by the nuns there. The priory was dissolved at the *Reformation*. Its ruins and Prioress's house still exist within the **Colman** grounds at Carrow.

CASTLE, THE

Originally a wooden structure built on a large mound with a dry ditch (the Castle has never been moated), it was designed by the **Normans** in 1067 as a stronghold from which a small number of French professional fighting men could control a large population of Anglo-Saxons who bitterly resented their presence. It was not built in stone until 1100 when a halt was called to the construction of the **Cathedral** and the masons moved across the city to spend two decades building in Caen stone a classic square Norman keep – 90ft square and 70ft high – of which the Frenchmen were immensely proud. They called it Blanchfleur – the white flower.

Overlooking the river and all the main roads, the Castle was the heart of the Norman power system. It was invested twice (in 1075 and 1217) but thereafter it declined in military importance and became the official residence of the Sheriff of Norfolk (originally the King's representative in Norwich) and the county gaol. It served in the latter capacity until 1887, when a new prison was erected on **Mousehold Heath** and the city bought the keep and prison buildings for conversion to a civic museum, which it remains today.

The Castle was refaced in 1837 using sandstone and limestone. Although the general treatment was felt at the time to be unsympathetic, the original design was followed closely and the Castle as we see it today looks very much as the Normans would have known it, although much reduced in overall area.

The twin gatehouses at its entrance, marking the position of the original drawbridge, were the site of many public executions in the 19th century. The scaffold was built between them and thousands of spectators would pack the old **cattle market** for a good view. The last public execution took place in 1867; thereafter the hangman did his work within the castle.

The Castle is a 'must' for every visitor to Norwich. Inside, it is possible to see what it must have been like when it was first built in stone, including the original 'fighting gallery'. A magnificent view of the city can be obtained from the roof and there are guided tours of the battlements and dungeons every day.

CASTLE MALL

This £100 million shopping complex, representing 350,000 sq.ft. of store space, was started in 1989 by developers Estates and General Investments between the old **Cattle Market** and **Timberhill**. It is the largest building project in the city since the construction of the **Cathedral** nearly 900 years ago. Due for completion late in 1992, it will include an underground car park.

CASTLE MEADOW

Once part of the castle ditch and an area where the cattle that provided milk and meat to the castle were grazed, this was a lane that stopped at the **Bell Hotel** until the arrival of the trams in 1900, when it was linked to Red Lion Street. It then became a narrow road barely accommodating two tramways but today it is one of the main routes through the city, offering an excellent worm's-eye view of the **Castle**.

CATHEDRAL, THE

Consecrated to the Holy and Undivided Trinity in the 12th century, Norwich Cathedral is one of the finest examples of ecclesiastical architecture in England and unique in northern Europe in its preservation of the *apsidal* plan behind the altar, an arrangement inherited from the early Christian worship in Roman *basilicas*. Thetford remained the see of East Anglia during the 30 years that followed the *Norman Conquest*. By 1094, however, Norwich had become the leading place in East Anglia and the Bishop of the day – **Herbert de Losinga** – decided that a new Norman cathedral should be built here. Much of the old Saxon burgh of Conesford was swept away as construction began in 1096. From the start the Cathedral was put in the charge of a community of up to 60 Benedictine monks. By 1119 (the date of de Losinga's death) the church had been completed as far as the east end of the *nave* and the masons transferred their activities to the **Castle**, which was completed in stone between 1120 and 1130. After this, work on the Cathedral and the monastic buildings resumed and was concluded around 1145. As there is no building stone in Norfolk apart from flint (and some carstone, also known as gingerbread stone, in the west of the country), great quantities of the finest quality French building stone were brought by water from the quarries at Caen in Normandy. It came by boat across the Channel, into the North Sea and then by river from the east coast. A canal was excavated from the **River Wensum** to the nearest point to the Cathedral building site. Here, at a special quay, the stone (much of it cut to size in Caen) and other materials such as Purbeck marble, local reeds, iron from France and Spain and timber from the Baltic, were unloaded. It was an amazing feat of organizational skill by 11th- and 12th-century builders.

The Cathedral was a monastic church until 1538, when Henry VIII ordered the *Dissolution* of the monasteries. Unlike the conventual church of the Blackfriars, however, it did not fall into disuse. Under a new constitution the monks renounced their monastic vows and became canons, petty canons and singing men (later to be known simply as clergy) and their head was called the Dean.

There is so much to see in the Cathedral that it all, literally, fills a book. If you are one of the 500,000 visitors each year, the best way to see and understand as much as possible is either to take a guided tour (there are guides on duty in the Cathedral every day) or to buy one of the excellent guide-books which are sold at the Cathedral shop. If you choose to find your own way round, here are a few of the treasures to look out for:

The magnificent west window (the best feature of an otherwise undistinguished west end) funded by **Bishop Alnwick** and built by his successor, **Bishop Lyhart**. The stained glass is Victorian.

The 15th-century lierne vaulted roof in the *nave*, also built by Lyhart through the master mason Reginald Ely, one of the architects of

King's College Chapel, Cambridge. The jointing of the ribs of the vaulting is marked by a series of carved and coloured bosses which are unique; there are 225 of them, telling in a kind of medieval strip-cartoon the story of God's involvement with man from the Creation to the Last Judgement.

The monument in the north aisle to **Osbert Parsley**, who served the Cathedral for 50 years through four reigns and all the upheaval of the *Reformation*.

The skeleton in the south aisle marking the grave of Thomas Gooding, a Tudor gentleman who insisted on being buried standing up on the principle that, when the grave finally gives up its dead, he has merely to step forward rather than waste time rising from his tomb.

The 15th-century choir stalls with the built-in *misericords* on which the monks could rest their bottoms for some relief during the eight services they attended each day (and night).

The wonderful carvings underneath each seat in the choir stalls, several of which are normally left tipped forward for visitors to see.

The unusual Flemish lectern in the presbytery, which is shaped like a pelican rather than the usual eagle and known as a pelican in its piety.

The Norman *apse* with its four chapels. The most modern of these – St Saviour's, the chapel of the Royal Norfolk Regiment – was built as recently as 1930.

The wooden Bishop's throne at the top of a flight of steps to the east of the altar. Beneath it are two pieces of ancient stone believed to be the last remains of the original 8th-century Bishop's throne used at North Elmham (site of the original See of East Anglia) and Thetford before the *Conquest*. (A cathedral is so called because it is a church containing the Bishop's throne or chair – in Latin, his 'cathedra'. This is the only cathedral north of the Alps always to have kept the throne in the original position. From here the Bishop gives the blessing on special occasions.)

The reliquary arch dating from 1278 and the more modern treasury on top of it.

The **Despenser** *reredos* in St Luke's Chapel, described as the greatest artistic treasure in East Anglia. It survived the destructive attention of the Puritans because it was used – upside down – as a table in the workshop of the Cathedral carpenter.

The pre-12th century effigy of a Bishop – perhaps of de Losinga himself – near St Luke's Chapel, which is believed to be the oldest Christian effigy in England.

The cloisters, which are the largest in any English cathedral, and took 130 years to build. They are unique in having an upper storey on three sides.

The view across the quadrangle formed by the cloisters, described recently by the Dean of Norwich as 'the finest in Christendom'.

The beautifully proportioned spire, at 315 feet the second highest in England.

The delicate 14th-century flying buttresses on the exterior of the presbytery, taking the weight of the roof and adding an air of elegance to the east end.

See also **St John's** Roman Catholic Cathedral.

(M)

ST CATHERINE'S CLOSE

Now the home of BBC East, this lovely Georgian house in **All Saints Green** with its fine Adam porch (a replica of the original) was built by John Morse when he became sheriff in 1779. He occupied it for more than 50 years.

CATTLE MARKET

The increasing amount of livestock brought

into the city during the 17th century forced the authorities to seek a permanent site for a cattle market to replace a scatter of markets throughout the city. Inevitably, a committee was appointed with a mandate to inspect the castle ditches, which were becoming an unofficial rubbish dump. As a result, an area to the south of the castle was designed for livestock sales and this remained the city's cattle market for three centuries. Eventually the approaches to this area became so congested that it was decided to open a new market outside the city centre and, in July 1960, stock sales moved to a 32-acre site at Harford, just off Hall Road.

The old cattle market place became a car park (due to be moved underground and the surfaces landscaped as part of the new **Castle Mall** development). A reminder of the original purpose of this area is to be found in the street names of Market Avenue, Cattle Market Street and Farmers Avenue.

(*M*)

CAVELL, EDITH (1865–1915)

If **Horatio Nelson** was the Norfolk hero, Miss Cavell must surely rate as the county's heroine. Daughter of the Vicar of Swardeston – a small village just outside Norwich – she was visiting her mother in the city's College Road when news of the German invasion of Belgium reached her and she immediately returned to the Brussels clinic of which she was head.

She allowed the hospital to be used not only as an escape route for wounded Allied soldiers but by young French and Belgian men seeking to join the Allied armies. It was not long before the Germans caught her; she was tried in secret and sentenced to death; and, despite frantic efforts by the American and Spanish ambassadors to Belgium, she was executed by firing squad in a rifle range just outside Brussels at dawn on 12th October 1915.

Her execution did much to sway neutral opinion against the Germans and helped to bring the United States into the war. The Allied propaganda machine exploited it to the full and within eight weeks of her death recruitment into the British Army – this was before conscription – had doubled.

After the war Edith was exhumed and, when the coffin was opened for identification, her body was found to be perfectly preserved. It was brought back to England for a service at Westminster Abbey and then taken by train to Norwich to be buried at **Life's Green** in the shadow of the **Cathedral**, on 15th May 1919. The memorial outside the **Maid's Head** was erected shortly afterwards and one feels that the inscription on it – Nurse, Patriot and Martyr – would have met, at least partially, with her approval.

She was a nurse by choice, a patriot by her very nature and a martyr by force of circumstance. This remarkable woman preferred to describe herself simply as 'a nurse who tried to do her duty'.

CHAMBERLIN'S BUILDING

A handsome Victorian corner building at the junction of Exchange Street and Lobster Lane, built in 1872 – some 40 years after this part of Exchange Street was created – to house the business of Chamberlin and Smith, wine and spirit merchants to the nobility and gentry. Its chief feature of interest is the royal arms carved in stone on the pediment at the top of the building.

The business had received royal patronage in 1884 from the Prince of Wales (later Edward VII) and had no hesitation in stating the fact in emphatic terms. At one time the Corn Exchange, built in 1861, stood opposite; as Geoffrey Goreham has remarked: 'Victorian Exchange Street marched rather than walked towards St Andrew's....'

CHAPELFIELD

This area of the city takes its name from the religious college of **St Mary in the Fields** which stood nearby and parts of which are incorporated within the **Assembly House** and the **Noverre** cinema. Bounded by Chapelfield Road, Chapelfield North and Chapelfield East are Chapelfield Gardens, the 8½-acre central public gardens of the city. It is an ancient open space, having been used as early as 1792 as an archery ground. Other uses have included a drill ground from 1854 (the old drill hall stood nearby until 1963 when it was demolished to make way for the roundabout at the top of Grapes Hill). At one time it was even the site of a reservoir. It became a public park in 1880. The splendid Victorian central bandstand rang to the strains of the Glenn Miller Band during the war and, in an earlier and less troubled age, Sir Alfred Munnings came to paint it. Look out for one of Norwich's most unusual artifacts, the **Gurney Clock**.

CHAPMAN, MARY (1647–1724)

See **Bethel Hospital**.

CHARING CROSS

The short stretch of road joining the end of St Andrew's Street with the junction of **St Benedict's** and Westwick Streets, chiefly notable now for the superb **Strangers Hall**. This was the centre of the weaving industry in the Middle Ages. Cloth-cutters and shearers would gather round the original cross waiting for employers to take them on. Known as Shearers Cross, it was demolished in 1732. The street had the same name but this was changed to Charing Cross, perhaps in imitation of the famous area of London.

CHURCHES, MEDIEVAL

It was always said that Norwich had a pub for every day of the year and a church for every Sunday. In fact, in medieval times there were 56 parish churches within the city walls and even today it has more than London, York and Bristol put together ... more, some say, than Rome itself. The actual total is 31. But for the destruction wrought by the Luftwaffe in the last war, there would be 36 – the same total as in 1707. Most were built, or rebuilt, in the 15th century by the city's newly-rich wool merchants in the majestic *Perpendicular* style and are characterized by square, embattled towers set at the western end, fine *clerestory* windows, two-storey porches and brass memorials within. With the notable exception of **St Peter Mancroft**, all are constructed from flint, the only local building stone. With so many churches, and only a handful of saints after whom places of worship were traditionally named, it was inevitable that there were many duplications, a problem of identity which was solved by adding the name of the parish (**St Peter Hungate, St Peter Parmentergate**) or a particular distinguishing feature (**St Martin at Oak, St Martin at Palace**). Other names have come down to us through the centuries – St Bartholomew, St Margaret at New Bridge, St Martin at Bale, **St Martin in Balliva** – but few traces remain of these once flourishing churches.

Inevitably, in a largely irreligious age, many of these churches have now been declared redundant and put to secular use by the Historic Churches Trust, which holds the freehold on 99-year leases from the city council. All the remaining medieval churches are described in this book together with an indication of whether they are used for religious or secular purposes.

Not included in the total of 31 is the former conventual church of the **Black Friars** purchased by the city from the Crown at the *Reformation*; the two famous Norwich free churches or chapels, the **Old Meeting House** and the **Octagon Chapel**; and the medieval churches outside the area of the old **city walls**, such as St Mary Earlham.

CHURCH HOUSE

Once the vicarage of **St John Maddermarket**, this historic building at the top of St

John Alley in **Pottergate** was saved from destruction in 1916, when in a state of considerable disrepair, by William Dibdin, who commissioned **George Skipper** to restore it.

Skipper found a drawing of a half-timbered gable which had existed on a vanished building nearby and made this a feature of the restoration. He uncovered the ground-floor windows and also the delightful little priest's doorway close to the church tower, which was preserved as originally built.

CHURCHMAN HOUSE

Described by English Heritage as the finest provincial town house of its era in England, this imposing Georgian building in St Giles Street was built between 1725 and 1740 by Alderman Churchman and became the home of Sir Peter Eade, physician and historian, who wrote the history of the parish of **St Giles**. Many mayors and sheriffs have lived here. At one time it housed the Norwich High School for Girls. It was restored at a cost of £400,000 during 1990 to become the Norwich Register Office.

CINEMA CITY

Not at all as ancient as it looks, this building in Redwell Street – formerly called Stuart and Suckling Halls – was built in 1924 by Ethel and Helen Colman when they were renovating the neighbouring **Suckling House**. Its chief claim to fame is that it was the venue, on 14th March 1927, for the first meeting of the Round Table, the association of young business and professional men founded by **Louis Marchesi** which is now an international movement. See also **Stuart and Suckling Halls**.

CITY HALL

Like it or loathe it (and it attracts strong feelings one way or the other), the city's premier administrative building is never ignored. Conceived by Charles James and Stephen Pierce (winners of a competition to find the best design), it stands on the site of the first Norwich bank and the place where James Smith sold the first Norwich ready-made shoes in 1792. It is built from Clipsham and Ketton stone and hand-made coloured bricks, and dominated by the 200-ft clock tower.

The architectural historian Sir Nikolaus Pevsner referred to it as 'the foremost English building of between the wars'. The down-to-earth local historian R. H. Mottram took a rather different view. He described it as having 'the proportions of a brick and the complexion of brown Windsor soup'.

The steps leading to the main doors are guarded by two heraldic lions, while the bronze doors themselves feature bas-reliefs by James Woodford, illustrating past and present industries of the city and key events in its history. The foundation stone was laid by the Lord Mayor in September 1936 and City Hall was opened by King George VI in July 1938.

ST CLEMENT

Believed to be one of the oldest churches in the city, St Clement the Martyr – although redundant – happily is still open for individual worship as a pastoral care and counselling centre. The *nave* is short and wide, the *chancel* lower and narrower, while the four-storey flint tower looks particularly tall and slender when viewed from **Colegate**. The church has neither aisles nor porches – just small entrance doors to the north and south. There is a burial ground on three sides but few memorials. Of those that remain, the best is a 19th-century box tomb which is particularly interesting as it represents the rebuilding of an earlier tomb erected by **Matthew Parker**, Archbishop of Canterbury under **Elizabeth I**, and contains the remains of his parents. Parker was christened in the church in 1504.

As if to compensate for its lack of exterior

Above: City Hall and market place.

Above: St Clement's tower behind Mischief Tavern and Fye Bridge.

Below: Colegate across St Clement's churchyard.

Left: Coslany Bridge.

Below left: City arms on Coslany Bridge.

Below right: Cow Tower at dusk.

memorials, the interior of St Clement's is fascinating for its monuments, mostly of two old Norwich families, the **Harveys** (merchants, manufacturers and bankers, who provided no fewer than eight mayors) and the Ives (wool merchants); both families were linked by marriage. We learn that Jeremiah Ives 'for three years endured the torture of the stone with invincible fortitude of mind', while John Harvey 'by his assiduous application and exact economy ... acquired an ample fortune' (is there a hint in the phraseology that he may have been a trifle mean?) The grand houses of both families still stand near the church, the Harveys' at Nos 18 and 20 Colegate and the Ives' opposite.

COLEGATE

Bounded at one end by **Magdalen Street** and at the other by Coslany Street/Oak Street, Colegate takes its name from its proximity to the point on the **River Wensum** where coal was unloaded from the vessels which had brought it from the east coast ports. Once the area where prosperous worsted merchants lived, it has some fine Georgian houses and doorways, notably the **Harvey** family houses at Nos. 18 and 20; two 16th-century flint buildings, including **Bacon House**; three fine churches (**St Clement, St George Colegate**, and **St Michael Coslany**), plus the two incomparable non-conformist chapels, the **Old Meeting House** and the **Octagon**.

Three remarkable Norwich women – the writers **Amelia Opie** and **Harriet Martineau** and the music teacher **Sarah Glover** – had associations with Colegate.

COLMANS

Jeremiah Colman had his original mill in Bawburgh, moving to Stoke Holy Cross watermill in 1814, where he began to manufacture mustard. When he died, the business was taken over by his nephew, Jeremiah James Colman, who moved it in 1850 to a new site at Carrow, just outisde the city walls, to be closer to the railway and the new **Thorpe Station**. By the latter part of the 19th century, Carrow Works was mainly engaged in the manufacture of mustard and starch, although some paper milling was also carried out – the name Paper Mill Yard still exists. Colmans now produce not only mustard but baby foods, soft drinks and a wide range of household goods as part of a major international company. J. J. Colman was a paternal employer with enlightened and benevolent views on treating his work force. He had a dispensary and a refreshment room built within the factory area and also constructed schools on Carrow Hill for the children of his employees, most of whom lived locally and had little access to public transport. The first works nurse in the country, Phillipa Flowerdew, was employed at Carrow. The Colman company has always been in the forefront of technology and it is interesting to reflect that the first telephone call from Norwich to London was made from the counting house at Carrow. The local newspaper was not impressed, reporting that it doubted if the system would develop.

See also the **Mustard Shop**.

COLTON, JOHN (d. 1497)

On his way to the city one night late in the 15th century, he lost his way and was in danger of drowning in the marshy surroundings, when he heard the bells of **St Giles on the Hill**. The sound guided him to **St Giles' Gate** and probably saved his life. In gratitude, when he died in 1497 he left to the church a piece of land, Colton's Acre, in Earlham Road (next to the present-day Mitre public house) on condition that a curfew be rung every night – a tradition that is still observed, using the Angelus bell, nearly 500 years later.

CONESFORD GATE

See **City Gates**

COSLANY

One of the four small Anglo-Saxon settlements from which Norwich grew, this is the area north of the **River Wensum** which became one of the busiest and noisiest in the city with a brewery, two ironworks, smithies, stables and factories. Today it is quiet again and given back to the residents, with two lovely parish churches – **St Mary** and **St Michael** (also known as St Miles) – standing within a few yards of each other.

Ⓜ

COTMAN HOUSE

Built in 1767 on the site of the old White Swan by Samual Pye (whose name is perpetuated in Pye Yard next to the house) and possibly designed by Robert Brettingham, who owned the White Swan, this imposing three-storey Georgian residence stands opposite the church of **St Martin at Palace**. It would probably be called Pye House but for the arrival here in 1823 of **John Sell Cotman** to make it his home and 'School for Drawing and Painting Water-colours: Terms one guinea and a half the quarter'. He remained until 1834. In 1937 the house was threatened with demolition under a slum clearance scheme but was saved and became a home for aged clergy. Eventually it was bought by Mrs Russell Colman and presented to the Norwich Amenities Preservation Society, who restored it.

COTMAN, J. S. (1782–1842)

Arguably the most celebrated of the artists who comprised the **Norwich School of Painting**, John Sell Cotman studied in London alongside Turner and Girtin and – like **John Crome** – earned his living mainly by teaching drawing to the wealthy as a 'polite accomplishment'. He spent most of his working life in Norwich – from 1806 to 1834 – the last 11 years in a house in **St Martin at Palace Plain** now called **Cotman House**.

His work was more sophisticated than Crome's and he was equally at home with oils and water colours. His best-known paintings include 'Fishing Boats in a Storm'. 'Silver Birches', 'Greta Bridge' and 'The Marl Pit'.

COW HILL

An unspoiled and largely undiscovered area of the city, starting in **Pottergate** and rising sharply to Upper St Giles, offering a good range of 17th-century houses with two 18th-century doorways on one side and the red brick and flint wall of **St Giles** churchyard on the other. There is a memorial to **George Borrow** at the base of the hill.

COW TOWER

Fifty feet high with walls up to six feet thick, this ancient tower stands like a lone sentinel on the banks of the **Wensum** where it bends to the west a few hundred yards north of **Bishop Bridge**. This area was originally called Cowholme and used for cow pasture – an oil painting by **Henry Ninham** dated 1840 shows a cow within the tower.

Built originally to allow the Prior of Norwich to exact tolls from shipping, the tower passed into the possession of the **Great Hospital**. It was conveyed in 1378 to the city, who promptly rebuilt it with bricks costing four shillings (20p) per thousand (the stone arrow slits by Robert Snape cost nine old pence, or around 3.5p, each). Thus it became the first structure in the city to be built entirely of brick.

It has had many uses over the years, including a church prison, lock-keeper's house and part of the city's defences, although it was never linked to the **city walls**. It was fired upon twice during **Kett's Rebellion** and the damage done to the battlements can still be seen. Cow Tower is one of the features of the city's riverside walk and well worth a visit.

Above: Davey Place.

Ⓜ

JOHN CROME (1768–1821)

Son of a tavern keeper in Upper King Street, 'Old Crome' as the Gurney girls called him was the leading artist in the **Norwich School of Painting**. He was poorly educated and, at the age of 12, became errand boy at the apothecary's shop and surgery of **Dr Edward Rigby** in **St Giles Street**. After an unfortunate incident in which he dropped a skeleton from an upper window on the heads of some medical students (who had earlier placed the same object in his bed), he was advised to seek alternative employment and became apprenticed to a sign writer, Francis Whisler, probably in nearby Bethel Street. Here he discovered his gift for painting and, under the patronage of **Thomas Harvey**, went on to establish a reputation as a painter of landscapes, inspired by the Dutchmen Hobbema and Ruisdael. He became drawing master to the **Gurney** family at Earlham Hall (now part of the University of East Anglia) and, as a successful artist, sold his works for as much as £100.

John Crome never lost the common touch and continued to accept commissions for inn signs, one of which can be seen in **Strangers Hall**. His best-known works were 'Moonlight on the Yare' and 'Postwick Grove'. Many of his major paintings are to be seen in the Colman galleries of the **Castle** museum.

The house where John Crome lived and worked off Colegate vanished long ago but his favourite tavern, the **Rifleman Ale House** in Cross Lane, is still to be seen, although no longer a pub. He is buried in the church in which he worshipped, **St George Colegate**. It is said that his last words, spoken to his son, John Berney Crome, were: 'John, my boy, paint – but paint for fame. And if your subject is a pigsty – dignify it!'

Ⓜ

CROSS-GROVE, HENRY (1683–1744)

The Norwich Post, published in 1701, was probably the first English provincial newspaper. Cross-Grove – who is commemorated by a green plaque at the Tuns public house in Unthank Road – edited the Norwich Gazette, which was set up in opposition six years later. A staunch Tory, he waged a war of words with the Whigs and was even indicted by them for treason but was acquitted. He was editor, and later proprietor, of the Gazette for 36 years and is credited with an innovation which is one of the most popular features in most newspapers today – the letters to the editor column.

Ⓜ

CROTCH, WILLIAM (1775–1847)

Born in Green's Lane, William was a musical prodigy – he played the organ before George III and the Prince Regent at the age of 3½, went to Cambridge at 11, had his first composition performed at 13 and was appointed Professor of Music at St John's College, Cambridge, at 22. He taught for many years at Oxford and was appointed first principal of the Royal Academy of Music at the (for him) advanced age of 47.

He never quite lived up to his early promise and today is virtually forgotten. Ironically, however, one of his musical pieces is broadcast every day. The Westminster chimes that precede the striking of Big Ben were composed by Crotch, based on a figure from Handel's 'Messiah'.

CROWN BUILDINGS

See **Hardwick House**.

Ⓜ

CUCKING STOOL

Situated at **Fye Bridge**, the cucking stool was used in Elizabethan times as an instrument of punishment. Offending women were tied on to it and lowered into the **River Wensum**. They were not drowned but probably had a good chance of being poisoned if they swallowed any of the noxious waters. It was written in 1814: 'This cucke-stool was the ordinary punishment of prostitutes, strumpets and common scolds ... women of the above description were to ride in a cart, holding in one hand a paper on which her accusation was inscribed, a brazen basin tinkling before her, and at one o'clock to be ducked in the river. Margaret Grove, a common scold, was the last that underwent this punishment, who in 1587, was sentenced to be three times ducked.'

The procession began at the **Bridewell** and the unfortunate woman was accompanied by a large band of citizens, for whom a public ducking no doubt did much to relieve the hard graft and tedium of everyday life. There was a similar stool at the village of Lakenham. Needless to say, it was not a form of punishment that was visited upon men.

Why cucking rather than ducking stool? Probably from the ancient word 'cucca' meaning (putting it politely) manure. It was the custom at one time for men or women who offended their neighbours to be tied to a chair before their own front door while choice pieces from the local dung-heap were thrown at them – hence cuke or cucking stool.

~D~

(M)

DAVEY, JONATHAN (1760–1814)

Throughout the 19th century, the authorities in all parts of Britain were haunted by the spectre of revolution. After all, it was only a few years since the French sent their King, Queen and leading aristocrats to the guillotine. No wonder that cries of 'Treason' rang out in the **Guildhall** council chamber when, one day in 1812, Alderman Davey announced: 'Gentlemen, I mean to put a hole in the King's Head.'

Davey was known to be a Baptist, a radical and a sympathizer with the French revolution. The council demanded either an explanation or a retraction. They got neither from Alderman Davey – merely the cryptic reply: 'Gentlemen, you must wait your time' – whereupon an armed guard was placed on his home night and day and constables were posted at the turnpike on the main road to London to apprehend potential assassins summoned by Davey to the city. Meanwhile, Davey – who must have had nerves of iron to go with his odd sense of humour – sat quietly at home saying nothing until, a week later, one of the city's great coaching inns, the King's Head in **Gentleman's Walk**, came up for sale at auction. Davey bought it and, true to his word, put a hole right through it to create a passage from the **market place** to the Castle ditches (now **Castle Meadow**). The result was Davey Place, Norwich's first pedestrian thoroughfare and still today very much as it looked in the 19th century. The hole in the King's Head also had the effect of creating an excellent new view of the **Castle** from the market place.

It is particularly appropriate that the council have created in modern times two major pedestrian areas close by Davey Place in **London Street** and Brigg Street/**Haymarket/Gentleman's Walk**.

Jonathan Davey was a shrewd businessman who joined with John Cozens and John Copeman to found Copeman's of Norwich and was one of the original directors of the **Norwich Union**. He used some of his fortune wisely to establish a lasting memorial to his name; two years later he was dead.

(M)

DAVEY PLACE

See **Jonathan Davev**

DESPENSER, HENRY (1341–1406)

The 'fighting Bishop' of Norwich, who seemed to spend more time on crusades than tending his flock, was a colourful and charismatic figure who, 600 years later, is remembered today through the Despenser *Reredos* in the **Cathedral** and the 252 panels in the ceiling of **St Helen's** church painted with the imperial eagle in honour of **Anne of Bohemia**. It was purely through his initiative that the **Peasants' Revolt** in Norfolk in 1381 was suppressed.

See also **Lidster, Geoffrey.**

DIRTY SHIRT CLUB

The **Rifleman Ale House** in Cross Lane (now a mission associated with the Sisters of All Hallows, Ditchingham) was one of the places where master weavers paid their outworkers on Saturday afternoons. The weavers came to the alehouse still in their working clothes and stayed to spend some of their earnings on liquid refreshment. That's how the Dirty Shirt Club gained its name. A ceremonial silver pipe was provided and new members of the club paid seven shillings and sixpence (37.5p) to smoke it. The Rifleman was a favourite pub of **John Crome**, who lived nearby.

DOLPHIN INN

See **Bishop Joseph Hall**.

DOUGHTY'S HOSPITAL

Founded by William Doughty in 1687, for 24 poor and aged men and eight poor and aged women, it now offers pleasant accommodation for old people in Victorian buildings and a modern extension in Golden Dog Lane, near **Magdalen Street**. In William Doughty's day, the residents were expected to be single and wear purple clothing. They were overseen by a Master who received two shillings (10p) a week. Their modern successors number 63 (including married couples), purple clothing is no longer de rigueur and a matron keeps a benevolent eye on them. William Doughty's portrait can be seen in the **Guildhall**.

D'OYLEY, REVD WILLIAM (1745–1814)

Born at Burgh Apton and curate in the Norfolk villages of Stratton St Michael and Flordon with Hapton, he was a poor parson who put his own comfort last when he saw that there was something to be done. D'Oyley's forte was to ride to outlying villages and solicit subscriptions to pay for road improvements; these included reducing a hilly road near Taverham to make it less steep and altering a sharp bend nearby. This accomplished, he then set himself up as a one-man road-widening scheme. The road in question was Brigg Street, between Rampant Horse Street and **Haymarket**, a notorious 19th-century bottleneck, where his green plaque is now to be found. Although nearly 70, he rode 12,000 miles collecting money locally to improve the road. He raised £400 but died before it could be used. Put into a trust fund, the money was eventually – 35 years later – used to carry out the work.

DRAGON HALL

Perhaps better known to Norwich people as the Old Barge Inn, this magnificent medieval house in **King Street** was built by Mayor and textile merchant Robert Toppes around 1450 and included a great hall, 88ft long and 22ft wide, as a showroom for his goods. The next occupant, Sir William Boleyn (grandfather of the ill-fated Anne) began a partitioning process which was completely to obscure the great hall and transform it into individual domestic dwellings. Many uses followed over the centuries – workers' cottages, rectory, butcher's shop, training centre, pub – and it has been owned by the city council since 1979.

When the Norfolk and Norwich Heritage trust was given the task of converting it into a heritage centre, one of its first tasks was to restore the great hall and open it to visitors. The superb original crown-post roof is now exposed and, while many of its intricate decorations have disappeared, one carved and painted dragon has survived to give its name to the hall. This is a monument to the mercantile history of the city and guides from the Heritage Trust will be delighted to show you round.

DUKE'S PALACE

The great palace of the Dukes of Norfolk stood at the junction of Duke Street and St Andrew's Street. The sixth Duke rebuilt it as his country seat and the 8th Duke demolished it in the mid-18th century. There was a pub on the site which represented the last remaining fragment but this was demolished in the 1960s. The site is now occupied by a multi-storey car park. See also **Howard House**.

~E~

ST EDMUND

This unpretentious church in Fishergate, recently restored and seeking a secular role, has much to commend it, including a curious arrangement of openings in the aisle arcade of differing heights and widths. There is, indeed, only one aisle, on the south side, with no *clerestory*. There is also a good timber roof and some fine late *Perpendicular* windows.

EDWARD VI SCHOOL

Known now as the Norwich School, it began its long life during the reign of the boy King in 1553/6 – in the place where it still stands in the Upper Close of the **Cathedral** – when the purchase of 'a seat for the common school' was recorded. Behind the **Carnary Chapel** and 18th-century frontage is a complex of modern facilities, including laboratories and workshops. Also part of the school since 1960 is the old **Bishop's Palace** to the north of the Cathedral. Probably the establishment of the school brought together various earlier educational establishments. Certainly, when **Walter de Suffield** founded the **Great Hospital** in 1249, it included a benefaction by which seven poor scholars nominated by the master of the Grammar School were to be given a daily dinner.

The school maintains close links with the Cathedral and provides 24 of its pupils for the choir. They practise in the Cathedral Choir School near the cloisters before and after the school day. Famous 'old boys' of the school include Sir Edward Coke, Lord Chief Justice in the reign of James I; the Elizabethan dramatist Robert Greene; and the Norfolk hero himself, **Horatio Nelson**.

In Nelson's day, the school – then the Royal Grammar School – had 45 pupils and two teachers. They worked from 7.30 am until noon and 2.00 pm to 5.00 pm, for which the headmaster, George Lemon, received a salary of £50 per annum.

ELIZABETH I (1533–1603)

Although Norwich was the great Tudor Queen's second city, she visited it only once – in the summer of 1578 in the 20th year of her reign. She entered through **St Stephen's**

Above: Elm Hill.

Above: Erpingham Gate from Tombland.

Below: Elm Hill from the rear.

Gate which had been elaborately decorated in her honour with red and white roses and the words:

Division kindled strife;
Blest union quench'd the flame;
Thence sprang our Noble Phoenix deare,
The peerless Prince of fame.

Although much of the city as she saw it is no more, there are a number of remaining buildings which are associated with her week-long visit, including the old **Bishop's Palace**, where she stayed; the largely medieval street of St John Maddermarket down which she progressed en route to the **Duke of Norfolk's Palace**; the house in **Elm Hill** (now the home of the **Strangers Club**) with the 20-light window from which she watched a pageant in her honour; and the **Great Hospital**, outside which the master of the Grammar School, Stephen Limbert, offered her a loyal and complimentary address in Latin.

ELM HILL

Probably the best-known street in Norwich, Elm Hill's quiet and cobbled charm captivates every visitor to the city. A busy thoroughfare in medieval times, setting for the homes and business premises of the rich and powerful in Tudor Norwich, it was a virtual slum at the turn of the century ('the steep and winding lane of Elm Hill, where the slum population stew and pig together down ancient courts and dirty alleys' ran a graphic description in 1901). Only the efforts of the Norwich Society saved it from demolition and redevelopment in the 1930s.

The magnificent Tudor buildings that were so close to collapse at the time stand sound and proud now, attractively colour-washed and offering a charming blend of 16th-century timbers, 17th-century dormer windows and Georgian façades. Elm Hill was almost completely destroyed by fire in 1507 and owes its appearance today to the fact that it was largely rebuilt in the following years. (Fires were a permanent hazard in the old walled city – **Francis Blomefield** recorded that, in another outbreak in 1507, 1,718 houses were destroyed in **Tombland** and the parish of **St Andrew's**). Unhappily the elm tree which gave the street its name no longer exists. The fourth of its kind, it finally succumbed to elm disease and was replaced in 1980 by a London plane tree. At the same time a water pump was placed nearby on the site of a pump first erected in 1639 at the time of an earlier replanting.

Elm Hill had the distinction of providing no fewer than 16 of its residents as mayors or sheriffs of the city. One of the reasons for its popularity among the merchants who made up the ruling clique was its easy access from **Quayside**, where the majority of water-borne imported goods came ashore.

Among the people who made their homes in Elm Hill were **Augustine Steward** and the **Paston** family (Nos 22–24), **Thomas Pettus** (Nos 41–43), the extraordinary **Father Ignatius** (No 14) and the **Friars de Sacco** (No 6). An excellent guide-book is available from many of the shops in Elm Hill.

ERPINGHAM GATE

Described as the finest cathedral gatehouse in England, it has stood opposite the west end of the **Cathedral** since 1420, when it was erected by **Sir Thomas Erpingham** to mark the great victory over the French at Agincourt five years earlier. It is the best of the four gates which guard the Cathedral precincts and makes an interesting contrast to its *Decorated* neighbour, the **Ethelbert Gate**, built over 100 years earlier and much restored in this century. Statues of the apostles and female saints rise towards heaven in the arch mouldings at the front of the gate; the east side is much plainer, with diagonal buttresses and a plastered gable decorated with the Erpingham arms.

The gateway suffered over the years by being altered or restored. **Francis Blomefield** complained in 1746 that the gate 'hath its beauty entirely spoiled by a chamber of wood fixed in the arch for a dwelling, which not only stops up great part of it but renders the sight altogether disagreeable'. Thanks to the sensitive restoration in 1955, in memory of John Henry Guy, a director of the **Mackintosh** and Caley companies, the Erpingham Gate is once again one of our finest *Perpendicular* monuments.

Ⓜ

ERPINGHAM, SIR THOMAS (1357–1428)

'Stout Sir Thomas', Shakespeare called him in *Henry V* – and if you want to know what he looked like, you can still see his effigy in stone, kneeling in prayer in a handsome niche in the centre of the flint-faced **Erpingham gateway**. The statue has been there since 1420 and has weathered remarkably well, presumably because of its canopy. His two wives (née Clopton and Walton) on either side were not so fortunate; their statues were exposed to the elements and are now unrecognizable. Sir Thomas was one of the city's most powerful and influential citizens in the late 14th/early 15th centuries. He was chamberlain to Henry IV and went with his son, Henry V, to France as commander – at the advanced age of 58 – of the English archers who did so much to win the Battle of Agincourt (25th Oct 1415). It was in thanksgiving for that crushing victory – French casualties between 7,000 and 10,000, English 100 – that the Erpingham Gate was built.

Sir Thomas lived in his palace just round the corner in **St Martin's Plain** until his death. The last fragment of that great house is a window from it incorporated into Spruce House opposite **St Martin's Church**. Sir Thomas was buried in his chantry chapel in the presbytery of the **Cathedral**. The chapel is long gone but you can still see his tomb, bearing the Erpingham arms.

ST ETHELDREDA

The last Norwich church to lose its traditional thatched roof (as recently as 1883), this is a building of many unusual and interesting features, which has been brought back to life by its use as a sculptors' studio.

The ancient tower is an attractive combination of flint and red bricks, its lower part a plain cylinder of flint and the upper part a flint octagon with brick angles and belfry surrounds. The whole is curiously short, rising only a little above the ridge of the *nave*. On the north side are the remains of a *Norman* arch with strips of Norman masonry – probably a string course – beside it. In the churchyard, hard up against the east end of the church, is the gravestone of Elizabeth Elvin, the parish midwife for 30 years, who died in 1849 aged 73, having brought into the world no fewer than 8,520 children. (For details of the record holder in this department, see the entry for **St Helen's** church.)

F

FINKELGATE

See – **Gate**.

FISHERGATE

Following the curve of the river from **Fye Bridge** Street to **Whitefriars**, old Fisher-

Above: Foundry Bridge.

Below: Fye Bridge.

Bottom: Fye Bridge by night.

gate was narrow and crowded with yards and courts fronted by decaying 17th-century homes. Much of it fell as part of Norwich's slum clearance in the 1930s but two original buildings survive – the church of **St Edmund** at the Whitefriars end and a fine, white twin-gabled house from the 17th century at the other. This is the former Duke of Marlborough public house which was de-licensed in 1972, restored and converted into flats and a garage.

FLYING ANGEL

For most of this century she has dominated the junction of **Castle Meadow**, Market Avenue and Bank Plain, looking down **Prince of Wales Road** from her lofty perch. She is the winged figure of Peace, sheathing the sword of war, on top of a column built of Aberdeen granite and Portland stone at a cost of £1,600. This is the city's memorial of the Boer War in South Africa at the end of the 19th century; inscribed on its sides are the names of 300 officers and men from Norfolk killed in that far-away and now largely forgotten conflict. In a war of more recent memory she was dubbed the Flying Angel by the young American servicemen who became such a familiar sight in the city and still return, as old men now, for their veterans' conventions.

FOREIGNERS

In Norwich parlance, a foreigner is anybody from another county or the next town or village – in short, from anywhere in the country but Norwich. Not a term used for people from overseas – they are called **Strangers**.

FOUNDRY BRIDGE

Named after the foundry which once stood nearby on the site of the modern **Hotel Nelson** (itself the successor to the 19th-century Great Eastern Hotel), this is the third bridge on this site. The first was built in 1810 and the second in 1844 (at a cost of £800) when **Prince of Wales Road** was constructed to provide access to the new **Thorpe Station** and an impressive entry to the city from the east. (Prior to this, the only routes across the river from that direction were by **Bishop Bridge** or Pull's Ferry.) The present Foundry Bridge was built in 1885.

FRIARIES

The concept of the various mendicant orders (that is, of religious communities whose members owned nothing but relied upon the charity of the people), most of which were founded in the early 13th century, came as a reaction to the wealth, power and property acquired by some of the older religious orders.

The citizens of Norwich found little of benefit from the remote and acquisitive Benedictine monks of the **Cathedral** priory, but they took readily to the friars, with their emphasis on preaching, teaching and healing, their self-imposed poverty and their identification with the people.

The city had within its walls no fewer than five mendicant orders – the **Friars de Sacco**, **Black Friars** (Dominicans), **White Friars** (Carmelites), **Grey Friars** (Franciscans) and **Austin Friars**. The only lasting reminder of these remarkable men, who suffered terrible losses during the plagues which regularly afflicted the city, and were eventually swept away by the tidal wave of the *Reformation*, is the great conventual church of the Black Friars now used as **St Andrew's and Blackfriars' Halls**.

(M)

FRIARS DE SACCO

Also known as the Sack Friars or Friars Penitential, they came to Norwich in 1258 from a newly-founded order in Marseilles and settled in the parishes of **St Andrew** and **St Peter**

Hungate. The order was not a success and was suppressed by Pope Clement V in 1307. The **Black Friars** applied for a royal licence to take over their site near **Elm Hill** and were permitted to do so on condition that they sheltered the one remaining Sack Friar, described as 'broken with age and nearly blind'. This was the basis for the construction of the Black Friars' conventual church, which remains as **St Andrew's and Blackfriars' Halls**. Remarkably, the early buildings of the Friars de Sacco, dating from between 1270 and 1307, still survive as the crypt coffee bar and Becket's Chapel. See also **Friaries**.

(M)

FRY, ELIZABETH (1780–1845)

Born Elizabeth Gurney in **Gurney Court**, off **Magdalen Street**, a member of the influential Quaker family which founded **Gurney's Bank**, she married Joseph Fry in 1800 and later became a Quaker 'minister'. Her greatest work, however, was as a prison reformer, campaigning for better conditions for female prisoners and those sentenced to transportation. As a girl, she was taught drawing by **John Crome**.

FYE BRIDGE

One of the city's five medieval bridges over the **Wensum** (London could only muster four over the Thames), Fye Bridge dates back as far as the 13th century, although the present structure was built in 1829 to a design by Francis Stone. It links two of the oldest Norwich streets, **Tombland** and **Magdalen Street**, and adjoins two more – **Quayside** and **Elm Hill**. In the 16th century it was the site of the city's ducking (or **cucking**) stool. The bridge was widened considerably after the floods of 1912.

~G~

(M)

GAOLS

There have been a number of prisons in the city over the centuries. The **Castle** was the county gaol from the 13th century until 1887; the dungeons of the **Guildhall** were used as a secure place for prisoners for many years and there were police cells there until as recently as 1987; the **Bridewell** was a prison/workhouse for beggars and vagrants in the 16th century; the site of the old Norfolk and Norwich Library and Tesco's opposite the Guildhall was used originally as a gaol, presumably to supplement the Guildhall facilities; and the City of Norwich gaol for 120 prisoners was built in 1827 at a cost of £22,000 just outside **St Giles' Gate**, complete with a treadmill which was operated by the prisoners (to grind corn) and four gallows. That prison was closed in 1878 and the area subsequently became the site for the Roman Catholic cathedral of **St John the Baptist**. The present-day prison on **Mousehold Heath** was built in the 1880s.

GARSETT HOUSE

See **Armada House**

GATES, CITY

The **city walls**, built between 1297 and 1334, included 12 great gates, many of them paid for by **Richard Spynke**, a rich merchant who thus freed himself and his successors from future service to the city. The more interesting of these gates are described elsewhere in this book. In a clockwise direction from the north, the gates were:

St Martin's Gate
St Augustine's Gate
Magdalen Gate
Barre Gate
Bishop Gate
Conesford Gate
Ber Street Gate
Brazen Doors
St Stephen's or Nedeham Gate
St Giles' Gate
St Benedict's Gate
Heigham Gate

In common with the walls, they fell into disrepair and were finally demolished between 1792 and 1808. Only a fragment of one of them – the Ber Street Gate – now remains.

- GATE

A number of Norwich streets end with the word 'gate', but this has no connection with the **gates** in the **city walls**. In this context 'gate' is a Saxon word meaning 'way or place of'. Obvious examples include **Colegate**, Cowgate, **Fishergate** and **Pottergate**. Less obvious are **Westlegate** (probably derived from wastels, or white loaves, which were made and sold in this street) and Finkelgate. A clue to the latter is that 'fink' in German means finch, so this may well have been an area in which caged birds were sold.

GENTLEMAN'S WALK

Situated to the east of the **market place**, running between **Haymarket** and Exchange Street, this was the area where Georgian gentlemen and their ladies would stroll on a Sunday to meet and exchange the latest personal and political news and gossip. Fronting on to it were many of the city's great coaching inns including the **Royal** (now the **Royal Arcade**, the upper part of which is the original hotel), the King's Head (demolished to make way for **Davey Place**), the Half Moon, the Bear, the Angel, the Tunns and the Lamb. The Walk was closed to traffic in 1987 for a trial period and then paved with flagstones and granite setts the following year (as were Brigg Street and Haymarket) to form the city's longest pedestrian precinct and one of its most colourful and crowded streets.

ST GEORGE'S BRIDGE

See **Blackfriars Bridge.**

ST GEORGE COLEGATE

It took more than 60 years to complete this fine church – the *nave* and tower first in 1459, the *chancel* in about 1498, the north aisle in 1505 and the south aisle in 1513. It stands at the junction of **Colegate** and St George's Street (once called Gildengate because it led to the **Gildencroft**).

This was the church frequented in the 18th century by the master weavers who lived in the fine large houses in Colegate. We are fortunate in having a reminder of those times, for this is the only church in the city to have retained many of its Georgian fittings, including a classical gallery at the west end supporting the little organ of 1802; the fine *reredos*; a magnificent pulpit with its sounding board and dignified pews made from the best wood of the original box pews.

There is the unusual terracotta tomb chest of Robert Jannys (mayor in 1517 and 1524) and – this being described as **John Crome's** church – the grave of Crome himself. Look also for the Victorian drinking fountain on the churchyard wall.

ST GEORGE TOMBLAND

Built like so many Norwich churches in the mid-15th century and once known as St George at the Gates of the Holy Trinity, this fine church stands in **Tombland** on a little triangle of grass which is thought to have been

Above: Gentleman's Walk.

Right: St Giles on the Hill.

Above: St Giles Street.

Below: St Gregory.

one of the burial pits for victims of the plagues which periodically swept the city. Interesting points of the exterior include a pretty blue clock on the south face of the tower and a *clerestory* of widely spaced windows with, surprisingly, walls of brick between.

The interior is not spectacular but the delicate pulpit, with tester and panel inlaid with ivory, is worth admiring, as is a window with a roundel of 14th-century glass depicting April – a man at the door of his house looks out on a shower of rain. There is also an unusual stone bread basket, from which bread was distributed to the poor of the parish. It is worth squeezing in beside the organ to see the babes in swaddling clothes on the **Anguish** memorial of 1617.

GILDENCROFT

A row of 12 Tudor cottages, with timber-framed frontages and lead-laced windows, facing the churchyard of **St Augustine** at the junction of Pitt Street and St Augustine Street. Like the **Guildhall**, they were saved from demolition by one vote in the council chamber. A £9,000 renovation scheme in the 1950s preserved them to perpetuate a corner of old Norwich-over-the-Water, the character of which has been so altered by the intrusion of the inner ring road.

ST GILES' GATE

Demolished in 1792, this was the main entrance to the city from the west and stood between what is now the entrance to Grapes Hill and Chapelfield Road. There was a leper house nearby.

ST GILES ON THE HILL

An imposing church dating from 1420 and distinguished by its 120ft tower (the tallest in Norwich), beautiful fan vaulting in the roof of the porch (again unique in the city) and an unusual *hammerbeam* roof within the lofty interior whose angels bear the coats of arms of England, France and Castile. Notwithstanding this, its greatest treasure is the eagle lectern of 1493, one of fewer than 50 pre-*Reformation* brass lecterns in existence. This one was probably made in the city.

For nearly 300 years the church had no *chancel*. The original was demolished in 1581 and not rebuilt until 1866. There are some excellent monuments, including two to the **Churchman** family who lived opposite, and interesting tablets and brasses. Look in particular for the brass of Elizabeth Beddingfield, before the Holy Cross altar; it bears the following noble inscription:

My name speakes what I was and am and have
A Beddingfield a piece of Earth a grave
Where I expect untill my soule shall spring,
For rayse and rayse out of the earth and slime
God did the first and will the second time.
Obit die 10 Maii 1637

Standing on an 80ft hill with its high tower, St Giles was the natural site for a warning beacon. The iron basket which contained the fire on the top of the tower – and which was probably used to announce the arrival of the Spanish Armada off the English coast in 1588 – can now be seen inside the church. See also **John Colton**.

ST GILES STREET

The Harley Street of 18th-century Norwich, this handsome road runs from **City Hall** to the church of **St Giles on the Hill** and onwards to become Upper St Giles. Most of the city's leading physicians had premises here and many fine 18th-century buildings are still to be seen. Here **John Crome** was apprenticed to **Dr Edward Rigby**, one of the founders of the **Norfolk and Norwich Hospital**. The Salvation Army building was formerly Brown's Hotel, where many of the stars of the Edwardian music hall stayed when playing at the nearby Hippodrome – now replaced, alas, by a modern concrete car park.

ST GILES TERRACE

Charming and easily overlooked little byway in the heart of the city, nearly opposite the Coach and Horses in Bethel Street, entered through a broad arch with the name of the Terrace inscribed in stone. Behind the arch is a row of early 19th-century houses, grouped together under a rising pediment, in the last of which lived **Joseph Stannard**, one of the **Norwich School of Painters**. He died in 1830 at the early age of 33 – if he returned today he would find St Giles Terrace much as he left it.

GLOVER, SARAH ANN (1786–1867)

One of the best-known songs in 'The Sound of Music' would never had been written but for Sarah Glover, who opened a school in a building behind the Black Boys public house in **Colegate** in the 1820s to teach scripture, writing, arithmetic, drawing, sewing and music to poor children. This unassuming Norwich woman devised the Tonic Sol-fah method of teaching the sight reading of music, based upon the notes of the major scale – doh, ray, me, fah, sol lah, te and doh.

The system was taken up by John Spencer Curwen, who was responsible for its publication and subsequent adoption throughout the country as a means of teaching amateurs of all ages to sight-read. By 1870 there were over 5,000 retained teachers of the Sol-fah system, with 1½ million pupils 'drawn mostly from the lower and middle classes'. Sarah Glover continued quietly teaching in the city and died at a ripe old age. The building which housed her school in Colegate no longer stands but the house where she lived in **Pottergate** can still be seen.

GOVERNOR'S TOWER

See the **Black Tower.**

GREAT HALL

An easy-to-miss medieval building in Oak Street, this is well worth a visit. It is a 15th-century wool merchant's home in the old Flower Pot Yard which is probably one of the oldest of its kind in the city, complete with long weavers' windows on the first floor. It was nearly swept away by the slum clearance programme in the 1930s, but Colonel Glendenning rescued it to demonstrate that 'old houses could be restored and have a century of useful life.'

The Germans had other ideas, however, for the bombing of the city in 1942 nearly removed it altogether but it was restored again in 1954 and now – a true survivor – it is used as a workshop.

GREAT HOSPITAL

One of the oldest foundations in the city, this is arguably the most ancient home for the elderly in the country. It was founded in 1249 by **Walter de Suffield**, Bishop of Norwich, as a home for 30 poor and decrepit chaplains (also expressed as distressed clergy) and as a place where 13 old folk and seven poor scholars could have a hot dinner and a place to warm themselves by the fire. Despite a pious inscription over its door in Bishopgate to the effect that:

King Henry the Eighth, of Noble Fame
Bequeathed this City this Commodious Place
With Lands and Rents he did endow the Same
To help decreped Age in Woeful Case

the Great Hospital only just escaped dissolution at the *Reformation* and was taken over by Norwich Corporation. Since the Municipal Reform Act, it has been independently run by Trustees.

It continues today as an old people's home in an unusual and perhaps unique setting, for it has its own church of **St Helen's**, with a tiny cloister leading to it, a fine refectory and a swan pit where – until as recently as 1938 –

Above: The Guildhall.

Below: Guildhall by night.

cygnets were fattened for the table. At the turn of the century a swan sold at a price of one guinea (£1.05p). It is now a popular haven for ducks.

Two queens visited here, **Anne of Bohemia** in 1383 and **Elizabeth I** in 1578. The latter drew rein at the hospital door to hear the master of the Grammar School read her an oration in Latin. Although extremely nervous, he delivered a loyal and complimentary address which pleased the Queen so much that she gave him her hand to kiss, saying: 'It is the best I have ever heard.' The Great Hospital may be visited by prior arrangement.

ST GREGORY

Overlooking a little square of grass (formerly the churchyard) which separates it from **Pottergate**, it has a charming clock in a classical surround over the door of the porch and several treasures within, including a fine octagonal font, the bowl of which is supported by eight angels, who look down upon eight monsters, apparently crushed beneath the stem, symbolizing the carnal desires of the flesh driven out by baptism. A large 15th-century wall painting in the north aisle was uncovered when the organ was moved in 1861.

One of the fascinations of St Gregory is the way in which the tall east end is built out over an alley, which slopes steeply down from Pottergate. This right of way seems originally to have been the bed of a stream and later part of a processional way round the church.

St Gregory is now a centre for music and the arts.

GREY FRIARS

A contemporary of St Dominic, St Francis founded the Grey Friars who arrived in the city in 1226 – the same year as the Dominicans – establishing themselves on a site east of **Castle Meadow**. Their extensive friary, which stretched as far north and east as the **Cathedral** precincts, has vanished beneath commercial development and the Victorian **Prince of Wales Road**. The only reminder is Greyfriars Road, which lies between the north end of **King Street** and **Rose Lane**. See also **Friaries**.

GUILDHALL

Henry IV granted Norwich its first Charter of Incorporation in 1404, which gave it the full status of a city and made it virtually self-governing, with the mayor directly responsible to the King rather than a provincial governor. To celebrate, the city's rulers (inevitably) formed a committee to recommend and design a major building to act as the city's administrative headquarters. As a result the Guildhall came into existence as by far the largest and most elaborate city hall ever built outside London. The name Guildhall is a little confusing. Although it had associations with the **Guild of St George**, it was never a merchants' guild hall but rather the centre of the city's government from the early 15th century until just before the last war. It was placed on the site of a small tollhouse dating back to *Norman* times, originally used to collect dues from the market traders, the only remains of which is the ancient undercroft beneath the east end of the building. Begun in 1407, the Guildhall was mostly built by conscripted labour. Workmen, citizens and **strangers** could be pressed by warrant to work on the construction from five in the morning until eight at night and all for nothing. Only the skilled craftsmen were paid, at the rate of sixpence (2.5p) per day. Meanwhile, the citizens were also forced to provide funds through taxation. With the exception of the **Cathedral** and the large friary churches, it was the most expensive structure to be built in the city. A final estimate of costs is around £500 at a time when the average income for the city from all sources was £120 p.a. By today's standards, the total cost would be in the region of £100,000.

It was largely finished by 1412 (although the

windows were not glazed until 1453) but 100 years later part of the roof and the treasury tower collapsed. It was not until 1534 that reconstruction began under the direction of that most energetic of Norwich citizens, **Augustine Steward**, who was also responsible for buying the **Blackfriars** church from the Crown.

His work was finished in 1537 at a cost of £208 and the building today looks much as it did then. The clock turret at the eastern end was added in 1850. One striking feature below the clock turret which is noticed by most visitors to the city is the flint and freestone chequerwork which may have been a medieval pun to remind people that a chequer table was in use within the building for the collection and counting of their taxes. Apart from this, the Guildhall is devoid of decoration, being built of flint and rubble faced with knapped flints laid in mortar and packed with flint chippings or 'gallets'.

Norwich nearly lost the building in 1908 when a proposal to demolish it was defeated by the casting vote of the mayor. Its function was taken over by the new **City Hall** in 1938 but it still serves the city today as the Tourist Information Centre and repository of the Norwich **regalia**. Guided tours of the Guildhall are available.

GUILD OF ST GEORGE

Founded in 1385, its original aims were religious, charitable and social – to honour St George and keep his feast day (23rd April), to pray for its members past and present and to offer alms to the poor and needy within the Guild. In 1417 it was granted a royal charter by Henry V, probably as a result of his acquaintance with prominent members of the Guild (including **Sir Thomas Erpingham**) who fought with him at Agincourt. The Guild gained important secular rights and privileges, protected by royal charter, and quickly developed into one of the most influential bodies in the city. It numbered over 200 members, among whom were some of the most powerful, wealthy and influential men and women in Norwich and Norfolk. The corporation gave it the top chamber of the **Guildhall** in 1486 to hold its meetings and keep its property.

The influence of the Guild declined after the formation of the Protestant government of Edward VI in 1547, although it continued to enforce its rules despite the abolition of its former powers. It stayed in existence until 1731 when its legality was finally challenged and the Company and Citizens of St George, as it was then called, surrendered its goods and possessions to the corporation. The Guild of St George, the Guild Days and the Norwich Snapdragon are inextricably linked. Further details are given under the heading **Snapdragon**.

GURNEY'S BANK

The Gurneys were originally prosperous wool merchants in the city who started adding simple banking transactions to other business they conducted with their customers. Gurney's Bank was formally established in 1775 when John and Henry Gurney entered into partnership.

Henry was succeeded by his son, Bartlett Gurney, who arranged for the bank to move to Redwell Street. The premises now form part of the site still occupied by Barclays in Norwich and known as Bank Plain.

Gurney's Bank rapidly expanded to Great Yarmouth in 1781, King's Lynn, Wisbech and Halesworth in 1782 and Fakenham in 1792, eventually operating throughout East Anglia. A series of amalgamations followed and, at the time of the merger with Barclays Bank in 1896, the firm's title was Gurney, Birkbeck, Barclay, Buxton and Company.

GURNEY CLOCK

Given to the city by Barclays Bank to mark the 200th anniversary in 1975 of the founding of **Gurney's Bank** in Norwich, this unique clock was designed and built by a master clockmaker, Martin Burgess, according to the ideas and principles of the 18th-century horologist John Harrison, who built the first successful marine chronometer. Unfortunately, it took so long to construct that the clock did not actually arrive for installation in **Chapelfield Gardens** until 1987.

Despite (or perhaps because of) its unpunctual beginning, it is in theory the most accurate mechanical clock in the world. Besides being an entertaining and useful addition to the city (you have to go to see it to understand it), the Gurney Clock is the only timepiece of its kind and of great horological interest.

(M)

GURNEY COURT

Courtyard off **Magdalen Street**, nearly opposite Golden Dog Lane, containing a medieval house refronted in Georgian times which was the birthplace of two remarkable Norwich women – **Elizabeth Fry** (née Gurney) in 1780 and the author **Harriet Martineau** in 1802.

GURNEY, ELIZABETH

See **Elizabeth Fry.**

GYBSON'S FOUNTAIN

A curious piece of old Norwich, also known as Gybson's Pump or Conduit, this 16th-century ornamented arch was erected in Westwick Street in 1576 by a brewer, Alderman Robert Gybson, when he was granted the rights to an old well which had delivered water in the parish of St Lawrence as far back as the 13th century. It was a condition that 'at his own charge in a conduit or a cock of lead he shall bring the water from the well into the public street for the ease of the common people and should maintain the same'. He fulfilled the condition and had the arch built around the conduit, complete with the city arms, the date 1578 and the inscription 'Vivat Regina' in honour of Elizabeth I, who visited the city during that year. The arch also features the following verses:

This water here caughte
In sorte as yowe se
From a spring is brorghte
Three skore foot and three.

Gybson had it sowghte
From St Lawren's wel
And he charge this wrowghte
Who now here do dwel.

Thy ease was his coste not smal
Vouchsafed wel of those
Which thankful be, his work to se
And there to be no foes.

Gybson became sheriff in 1596 but fell out with the mayor and for 'reproachful, scornful, contemptuous and foul speeches and unfitting behaviour' he was deprived of his aldermanship and disfranchised in 1602. He died in 1606 and his bones lie in the *chancel* of **St Lawrence the Martyr**, just across the road from his fountain, which is well worth seeking out within the old **Anchor brewery** precincts.

~H~

(M)

HALL, BISHOP JOSEPH (1574–1656)

Appointed Bishop of Norwich in 1641 as the country rushed headlong towards the Civil War, his strong Royalist sympathies in the heartland of Cromwell's Eastern Association made him a marked man among the Puritans.

Above: Bishop Hall's Palace, now the Dolphin Inn.

Left: Hampshire Hog cottage.

With 11 other Bishops of similar opinions, he was sent to the Tower of London charged with treason but released on bail of £5,000 after the charge was dropped.

Back in Norwich worse awaited. He was forced out of the **Bishop's Palace**, had his property and possessions seized and then watched helplessly as Cromwell's men desecrated the **Cathedral**, destroying everything that they regarded as being idolatrous. (Lodged in the north side of Bishop Goldwell's tomb in the presbytery is a musket ball which is probably a relic of that day.) Prevented from using his Cathedral and without a Palace, the Bishop established himself just outside the city in the village of Heigham, taking a flint and stone house built in 1587, with Jacobean bays added in 1615. Although Norfolk was a Parliamentary area, the people revered him – to them he was Bishop Hall and his new house was the Bishop's Palace. He didn't live to see the restoration of the monarchy, dying in 1656. He is buried in St Bartholomew's Church, Heigham. His palace lives on as 258 Heigham Street. Badly damaged during the Second World War, it has been restored and now bears the name of the Dolphin Inn.

HAMPSHIRE HOG YARD

Site of one of only five remaining thatched properties in Norwich, this is situated off St Swithin's Alley between St Benedicts and St Swithin's Road. For many years it was the Hampshire Hog public house, whose landlord, John 'Licker' Pratt, defeated **Jem Mace** in a two-hour bare-knuckle contest at Drayton in 1850.

(M)

HANSARD, LUKE (1752–1828)

The name Hansard for the official proceedings of the Houses of Parliament, published by Her Majesty's Stationery Office, has its origins in the parish of **St Mary Coslany**. It was here that Luke Hansard was born. In nearby **Magdalen Street** he was apprenticed to the printer Stephen White at the sign of the Bible and Crown. Young Luke went to London with a guinea in his pocket and a determination to become a man of substance. By the time he was 22 he was working for John Hughs as a master printer, responsible for an unofficial account of the proceedings of the House of Commons published by William Cobbett. In due course, Luke married into the family, became the owner of the printing business and died worth £80,000.

His printing works continued to publish the House of Commons reports until 1889, when the role was taken over by the Stationery Office. The name Hansard was not officially adopted for the proceedings until 1943. By an extraordinary coincidence, when the Stationery Office moved to Norwich in the 1960s it occupied new headquarters within a stone's throw of the parish where Luke Hansard was born and the street where he learned his trade.

HARDWICK HOUSE

A substantial 19th-century building at Agricultural Hall Plain designed by P. C. Hardwick and built in 1865 at a cost of £13,000 by Sir Robert Harvey as a bank. It was the scene of a near-riot in 1870 when depositors besieged its doors as news spread that Sir Robert had speculated unwisely on the result of the Franco-Prussian war and the bank had failed. While a fellow director told them that they would get some of their money back, at the rate of 10s 6d (52.5p) in the pound, Sir Robert shot himself. Once again he got it wrong – it reputedly took three attempts before he was successful. The bank – whose symbol of a crown still dominates the pediment of the building – was then merged with **Gurney's**.

To most Norwich citizens, Hardwick House (also called the Crown Building) is the old head post office, for it played this role from 1870 to 1969. Anglia TV now occupy it, having linked the building to the adjacent **Agricultural Hall** and added a modern office at the back.

When excavations took place prior to building, the remains of a previously unknown Anglo-Saxon church were discovered.

Ⓜ

HARVEYS

One of the most influential Norwich families whose name recurs constantly in the history of the city, the Harveys founded their fortunes on the wool trade and supplied a total of eight mayors and seven sheriffs. Not all Harveys were successful, however – as already mentioned, Sir Robert Harvey shot himself in 1870 when his bank failed. The brothers Robert and Thomas Harvey, who flourished in the 18th century, are commemorated by two particularly fine adjoining Georgian houses in **Colegate**, Nos 18 and 20, opposite the **Octagon** chapel. The doorcase of No 18 is said to have come from the **Duke of Norfolk's Palace** at Duke Street. Both houses were built around 1730.

HAY HILL

Open space west of **Haymarket**, chiefly notable for the statue of **Sir Thomas Browne** which was unveiled in 1905 and was resited in its present fountain setting in 1972.

Ⓜ

HEARNE, RICHARD (1908–1979)

Actor, entertainer and creator of the popular children's TV character Mr. Pastry, he was born at 21 Lady Lane (now called – for reasons best known to the city council – Esperanto Way) on the site occuped by the **Central Library**.

ST HELEN

It is not often that you see a church with chimneys, but this unusual sight awaits in **Bishopgate**. St Helen's is part of the fascinating cluster of buildings which comprise the **Great Hospital** and serves as a chapel for the hospital and a church for the parish. It was erected in 1380 by **Bishop Henry Despenser**.

Anne of Bohemia and her king, Richard II, took an interest in the church and Despenser had 252 panels in the wooden roof of the *nave* painted with a double-headed-eagle – the symbol of her father, the Holy Roman Emperor, Charles IV – to commemorate their visit to the city in 1383.

While the *nave* is original, Bishop Goldwell had the remainder rebuilt about 100 years later and then, towards the end of the 16th century, the church was divided up to provide wards for the inmates of the Great Hospital. The *chancel* was divided horizontally into two storeys and became the women's wards and the nave was similarly treated to provide men's wards – hence the chimneys in the roof leading from the fireplaces below. The space between the new wards was sealed off and remained as a place of worship.

The most interesting architectural feature within the church is the lierne vaulted roof of the transept, with beautifully carved and coloured bosses at the intersections of the ribs, similar in style to the vaulting in the roof of the **Cathedral** nave. There are also excellent Georgian box pews, including one erected by **William Ivory** in 1780, in order to be 'convenient for his family and servants'. The churchyard contained the grave of Phoebe Crew, midwife, who died on 28th May 1827, aged 77, and is alleged to have brought 9,730 children into the world. (See also **St Etheldreda**.)

ST HELEN'S HOUSE

Set between the **Adam and Eve** and the **Great Hospital**, in **Bishopgate**, this was the home of **Thomas Ivory,** the city's leading 18th-century architect, built on land granted to him on a 99–year lease by the hospital committee. He lived here from 1756 until his death in 1779, whereupon his son, **William Ivory**, became the occupant. It has been surmised that William enlarged the house and completed it as it is today.

HERMITAGE, THE

Another of the five remaining thatched dwellings in the city, this fine house in **Bishopgate** is known to have existed in the 16th century and has 13th-century mullioned windows.

Ⓜ

HOG HILL

The old name for Orford Hill, between **Red Lion Street** and **Timberhill**, so named because it led to the swine market in **All Saints Green**. It was retitled in the 18th century in honour of **George Walpole**, 3rd Earl of Orford, who contributed generously to a public subscription to improve the area.

HOLM-STRETE

In medieval times Holm-strete led from the Bishop's Gate on **Bishop Bridge** to **St Martin at Palace**. Today the great gate no longer exists and the name Bishopgate has been given to Holm-strete. Confusing, isn't it?

Ⓜ

HOSPITAL, NORFOLK & NORWICH

Founded in 1771 as the first general hospital of the modern kind in Norfolk, it was built on three acres of land just outside **St Stephen's Gate**, leased by the **Great Hospital** at £6 a year with the provision that the rent should be doubled if the premises ceased to be used as a hospital.

The architect was **William Ivory**, who supervised the construction for four years without charge. While primitive by modern standards, with no drains, no piped water, no trained nurses and only one resident doctor, it nevertheless saw some major steps in health care because here, for the first time, visiting consultants became familiar with the diseases of the poor. It became a pioneer hospital; its surgeons were noted for their skill in the treatment of gallstones (more common in Norfolk than any other county) and were among the first in England to use anaesthetics and antiseptic techniques. That early building, most of which still stands, was followed in 1883 by a new hospital on the same site, designed by Edward Boardman and T. H. Wyatt, which is also still in use, although the main hospital is now housed in modern tower blocks behind – these date from 1965.

Ⓜ

HOWARD HOUSE

Built by Henry Howard, later 6th Duke of Norfolk, as a garden house on land previously occupied by the **Austin Friars** in **King Street**. It was reported at the time (around 1660) that: 'Mr Henry Howard hath lately bought a piece of ground of Mr Mingay, by the waterside in Conesford, which he intends for a place of walking and recreation and for a garden'. He clearly achieved his intention but the small garden to the east is all that remains of the large orchards and pleasure grounds created by Howard which stretched to the river. For many years after his death this was known as 'My Lord's Garden'.

As befits a garden house, it has a sundial, situated high up on the wall overlooking the remains of the garden, but it is not original, being dated 1840. Parts of the house may be 16th century and there is a fine Jacobean staircase.

HUNGATE STREET

The original name for Princes Street. It stretched from St Andrew Broad Street to **Tombland**, through the parish of Hungate. The name is believed to be a corruption of Houndgate, for this was the area where the early Bishops of Norwich kept their hunting dogs. Their hunting ground was Thorpe Wood, to the east of the city.

Above: Jarrolds' store.

Below: St John's R.C. Cathedral.

~I~

(M)

IGNATIUS, FATHER (1837–1908)

Norwich has known few characters as controversial and inexplicable as Joseph Leycester Lyne, a self-appointed monk who arrived in 1864 in an attempt to re-establish Benedictine monasticism in a city none too keen to embrace it. He established the Priory of St Mary and St Dunstan in **Elm Hill**, comprising initially himself, one other brother and a dog, and imposed strict Benedictine discipline. There were up to eight services a day, the first at 2.00 a.m. Surprisingly he gained a number of converts, including the Rector of **St Lawrence the Martyr**, but he incurred the enmity of many more people than he won over. He seemed, however, to be possessed of extraordinary powers. A woman who cursed him in the street fell dead in her doorway. Another mocked his tonsured head, only to see her child's hair fall out. It refused to grow again until Father Ignatius laid his hands on the boy's head. Finally, when a churchwarden who had complained about him to the Bishop also fell dead, a mob descended on his monastery intent on burning it to the ground, only to be dispersed by a sudden, violent and unpredicted thunderstorm.

Ignatius's autocratic ways and lack of financial acumen finally caused the order to fall apart in 1866. Ignatius moved on and pursued his independent path for 42 years, mainly through a more successful monastery which he established in the Brecon mountains. Reminders of this remarkable man can still be seen. The door to his monastery fronts on to Elm Hill while to the left of the building is Monastery Court leading to the large red-brick chapel which he built but never completed. It is now used as a school for graphic design.

IVORY HOUSE

Fine Georgian house in **All Saints Green** built by **Thomas Ivory** as a horse artillery barracks in 1772. It now forms part of the City College.

(M)

IVORY, THOMAS (1709–1779)

The leading Norwich builder and architect in the 18th century he was responsible for many fine buildings in the city, a number of which are still standing. His masterpieces were undoubtedly the **Assembly House** (1754) and the **Octagon Chapel** (1756). He rose high from humble beginnings, having been appointed carpenter to the **Great Hospital** in 1751. He became a joiner, a builder and an architect of genius and still found time to export Norwich cloth in exchange for timber and deals. He was for some years the proprietor of the **Theatre Royal**, the original of which he built in 1758.

IVORY, WILLIAM (1746–1801)

Like his father, **Thomas Ivory**, he was an architect and completed his father's work at **St Helen's House** in **Bishopgate**. He designed the first buildings for the **Norfolk and Norwich Hospital** and supervised the work without charge for four years.

~J~

JAMES STUART GARDEN, THE

Probably the least known of the city's parks, this pleasant little garden, reached via a Jacobean-style gateway at the junction of Recorder Road and St Faith's Lane, is a memorial to the husband of Laura Colman, daughter of **J. J. Colman**. James Stuart was born in Scotland in 1843 and became a Member of Parliament whose great concern was to bring education to the masses and overcome the high rate of illiteracy which prevailed among the working-classes in the 19th century. The idea of a memorial garden in his name was first suggested before the First World War but it was not completed and officially opened until 1922.

ST JAMES HILL

An excellent point for viewing the city, between Ketts Hill and Gurney Road on the fringe of **Mousehold Heath**. While the **Cathedral, St John the Baptist** Roman Catholic Cathedral and the **Castle** can hardly be mistaken, other prominent buildings are identified with the help of a large plaque erected at this point in memory of the local novelist and historian, Ralph Mottram, who had an interest in the history and appearance of the city. He died in 1971.

ST JAMES POCKTHORPE

Long situated in a slum parish whose inhabitants were among the poorest in the city, St James has a curious brick tower that stands actually on, rather than beside, the church and is shaped like a cube, with a battlemented octagon on top. Look, too, for the tiny door on the north side. Redundant, like so many of Norwich's pre-*Reformation* churches, St James nevertheless continues to serve the city, for it has been converted into an intimate and delightful puppet theatre.

JARROLDS

The Jarrolds have long been associated with Norwich in both an administrative and a mercantile sense. The family owns a department store, designed by **George Skipper**, in **London Street**, and a printing works in Whitefriars which is a graceful example of early Victorian industrial architecture, described in more detail under the entry for the Norwich **Yarn Mill**.

JEWS

The development of Norwich during the 12th century, when there was an explosion of building of all kinds, was largely financed by the Jewish community, which probably came to the city from northern France and the Rhineland. Christians were not allowed to lend money, but Jews were allowed to do little else. They were protected by royal officials because they were legally the King's chattels. Most of them lived in the Jewry in White Lion Street and the **Haymarket** area, within easy reach of the **Castle** precincts should anti-semitism become a problem. (In 1144 the Jews were accused of the ritual murder of a boy – later known as **St William** although never officially canonized – and were taken into the Castle by the sheriff to protect them from the wrath of the citizens).

The Jewish community declined in the late 13th century through royal exploitation and popular persecution. Eventually, in 1290, all English Jews were expelled from the country; at that time the Norwich Jewish community had declined to 17 impoverished households. There was probably a synagogue in the area of Dove Street in the 12th and 13th centuries. The present-day synagogue is in Earlham Road.

See also **Jurnets**.

ST JOHN THE BAPTIST

Many people do not realize that Norwich has not one but two great cathedral churches. The Roman Catholic Cathedral of St John in Earlham Road was built as an act of thanksgiving for his marriage and other blessings by the 15th Duke of Norfolk and designed by George Gilbert Scott and his brother, John. Their idea was to fill the gap in the city's ecclesiastical architecture by building an example of pure *Early English Gothic*. They certainly succeeded in their ambition for there can be no finer example of Victorian Gothic revival anywhere in England, and few so dramatically positioned.

Situated on the high ground previously occupied by the **City of Norwich gaol**, just outside the old **St Giles' Gate**, it began with the laying of the foundation stone in July 1884. A decade later the *nave*, baptistry and memorial chapel were opened but it was not until 1910 that the church was completed. Because of its setting, the nave is on a level with the base of the spire of the **Cathedral**, which means in turn that there is a magnificent view of the city for those who brave the 228 steps to the top of the tower.

St John did not actually attain its present status until 1976, when Pope Paul VI announced the establishment of a new diocese and designated the church as its Cathedral. It is the largest Catholic church in the country after Westminster Cathedral.

ST JOHN MADDERMARKET

Standing at the top of the narrow **Maddermarket** Alley, which pierces its beautiful tower, this is the church where the Dukes of Norfolk would have worshipped when visiting their great palace nearby. Indeed, Margaret, Duchess of Norfolk, who died in the Duke's Palace in 1563, is buried here. Look for the four evangelists in stone on the parapet of the tower and the magnificent east window filled with Victorian glass. No longer used for Anglican services, the church has been taken over by the Redundant Churches Fund which plans to restore it and open it to the public.

ST JOHN DE SEPULCHRE

The church of St John the Baptist and of the Holy Sepulchre, to give it its full name, was the first to be seen by travellers entering the city through **Ber Street** gates. Standing high on the Ber Street ridge, it has one of the most striking stone-and-flint towers in Norwich – a landmark which dominates the southern end of the street. It is an aisleless church with a small *chancel*, a pretty two-storeyed north porch and *transepts* on either side. The tower is reinforced by diagonal buttresses that step inwards at each of its four stages to reach a battlemented parapet to which small pinnacles were added in 1904. Like most of the city churches, it is largely *Perpendicular* in style and thus dates from the 15th century.

Inside are two interesting brasses – one to a brother and sister (Winifred and John Brown) holding hands, the other one of the few *palimpsests* in the city. It displays an engraving of a husband and wife, dated around 1535, on one side and, on the other, a much earlier engraving of a monk – possibly an anchorite who lived in a hermitage in the churchyard.

The church is now used by the Orthodox community of Norwich.

ST JOHN TIMBERHILL

Formerly known as St John at the Castle Gate, this attractive little church at the junction of Timberhill and Golden Ball Street – one of the few in Norwich without a tower – was the burial place of those who died in the **Castle** gaol, as was the now destroyed **St Michael at Thorn**. The church as we see it today fulfils the vision of the Revd. Edward Ram, who became vicar in 1871 and remained for 47 years. He rescued it from neglect and adapted it for modern use. There is a nice stone bell-tower which, like the slate roof over the *nave* with its little dormer windows, is unmistakeably Victorian. The interior is small and well cared for, with the only *rood beam*, with crucifix and attendant figures, remaining in a Norwich church. This one was carved in Oberammergau and installed in 1890.

From an earlier age there are two fine candelabra (one German dated 1500, the other from around 1700) and one of the best wall tablets in the city, in which a cherub mourns the passing of Robert Page (1778).

ST JULIAN

This old church was situated in one of the worst slum areas of the city, sandwiched between the breweries beside the river and the butcheries of **Ber Street**. Today the area is very different, comprising pleasant modern housing and offices, and so is the church, for the original was destroyed by enemy bombing in 1942.

It was probably only its association with **Julian of Norwich** that caused the church to be rebuilt, for there were no fewer than four others standing within a quarter-mile of it. The architect, A. J. Chaplin, did a marvellous job in rebuilding the church in 1953, including a reconstruction on its original site of Julian's cell, which had fallen down in the 16th century.

The whole atmosphere of St Julian is heightened by the way that Chaplin incorporated features from earlier times into the modern fabric. The round tower – now half its original size – is Saxon. High in the north wall of the *nave* are two circular windows which are almost certainly Saxon and have certain affinities with embrasures in the flint wall fronting the west cloister of the **Cathedral**. There is a particularly fine *Norman* doorway to Julian's cell which came from **St Michael at Thorn**, destroyed on the same night as the church of St Julian and never rebuilt. The cell itself has two pieces of flintwork near the ground which formed part of the original foundations.

The greatest treasure, however, is the font, dating probably from Julian's lifetime. It is one of the best in the city and was placed here from **All Saints** when it was declared redundant in 1977. After the Cathedral and the mighty **St Peter Mancroft**, St Julian must rank as the most visited church in the city, for followers of Julian of Norwich come here from all over the world on pilgrimages to the place where she lived and taught for 40 years.

(M)

JULIAN OF NORWICH (?1342 – ? 1415)

Did the mystic give her name to the church, or the church to the mystic? Nobody really knows but it seems likely that the church of **St Julian** was dedicated to Julian the Hospitaller, patron saint of ferrymen, when it was established in pre-Conquest times. Julian of Norwich (Dame Julian, Mother Julian or Lady Julian, as she is variously known) became an *anchoress* here in 1373 and probably took her name from the church.

The reason that Julian's name has come down to us across six centuries is that she left behind a permanent memorial of her devotion. During a serious illness, just prior to her becoming an anchoress, she received a series of 16 'showings' of the Lord. For the next 20 years she meditated on these and then recorded them, and what she perceived to be their meanings, in a book entitled 'The Revelations of Divine Love'. It was the first known book written by an English woman and is now acknowledged throughout the Christian world as one of the great classics of spiritual literature.

Her cell was a small dwelling attached to the church with a window into the choir, through which she could hear the Mass and receive Holy Communion, and another on to the street so that she could counsel visitors. One such pilgrim – Mary Kempe – recorded a visit to 'Dame Jelyan' in these words: 'Much was the holy dalliance that the anchoress and this creature had by communing in the love of our Lord Jesus Christ.' Little is known of Julian's early life and even the date of her death is not recorded – we only known that she was an anchoress for over 40 years and lived into the early part of the 15th century. She claimed to be unlettered but may well have been educated by the nuns at **Carrow Priory** and may even have been a member of their community. From her writings we know that she had her 16 visions on 8th May 1373 and became an anchoress when 'thirty and a half years old'. Her rebuilt cell at St Julian's church is a quiet and holy place for the pilgrims who come here from all over the world to pay tribute to a remarkable Norwich woman.

JURNETS

This was the family who did most to finance the early growth of the city – in the 13th century Isaac Jurnet was thought to be the richest Jew in England. His father built himself a strong stone house in **King Street** in 1175, specifically designed to withstand attack by the mob and with an undercroft to store his riches. It still exists as the **Music House**, the oldest dwelling house in the city.

Jurnet senior acted as the agent of the Bishop of Norwich and financed extensions to the **Cathedral**. The family lived in King Street, until around 1240.

~K~

Ⓜ

KEMP, WILL (d. ? 1608)

Actor and friend of another William (he performed Shakespeare's plays at the Globe and Fortune Theatres in London as a member of the Lord Chamberlain's Company), he achieved the extraordinary feat in 1599 of Morris dancing between the two main cities in the realm – London and Norwich.

His journey was the result of a bet and he was sufficiently confident to back himself at odds of 3 to 1. He set out from the Mansion House, accompanied by three gentlemen with extremely theatrical names – Tom Sly to provide the music with tabor and pipe, his manservant William Bee and George Spratt, who acted as referee. After nine days of actual dancing on appalling roads (they have improved somewhat since then, but not a great deal) he arrived at **St Giles' Gate**. Finding the crowds there rather small, and being a typical actor, he retired to spend the night at an inn outside the city walls and returned to the gate in the morning. By then the reception was more to his liking and he entered the city in triumph.

He danced down **St Giles Street**, turned left into Dove Street (then called Holtor Lane) and concluded his epic journey by jumping over the wall of the churchyard of **St John Maddermarket** to reach the home of the mayor, Roger Weld. In addition to winning his bet, Kemp received £5 in Elizabethan angels from the mayor, who nailed his buskins (dancing shoes) to the **Guildhall** at the same height as his final leap.

Will Kemp wrote an account of his journey, entitled 'Nine Daies Wonder' (although his nine days of dancing were spread over many weeks). His epitaph in St Saviour's Church, Southwark, reads:

Welcome from Norwich, Kempe all joy to see,
Thy safe return morriscoed lustily.
But, alasse, how soon thy morrice done!
When Pipe and tabor, all thy friends be gone.
Then all thy triumphs, fraught with streams of mirth
Shall be caged up within a chest of earth;
Shall be? They are, th'ast danced thee out of breath
And now must make thy parting dance with death.

KETT'S REBELLION

For six weeks in the summer of 1549, an army of 20,000 yeoman farmers, led by **Robert Kett**, entrenched itself on **Mousehold Heath** and attacked and occupied the city in protest against increased rents and, specifically, the enclosure of common land by the local gentry. It was the greatest insurrection the county has ever known and it took two royal armies to suppress it.

The first, under the command of the Earl of Northampton (not one of history's most notable soldiers) arrived from London on 31st July, nine days after Kett's men had fought their way into the city. The following day Northampton's army was soundly trounced in the battle of **St Martin's Plain** and his second-in-command, **Lord Sheffield**, was killed by one of the rebels, named Fulke, who was – appropriately – a butcher by trade.

The rebels remained in control of the city for the next three weeks, maintaining their camp on Mousehold, until a far more formidable commander, in the shape of the Earl of Warwick, arrived, followed soon after by 1,100 German mercenaries.

The rebels withdrew from the city to their camp and from there Kett led them into battle on 27th August in the area of Dussindale. Removed from the impregnable heights of Mousehold, the untrained countrymen were no match for the combined cavalry, infantry and artillery of Warwick's professionals and, in a three-hour battle, they were cut to pieces. Many of the leaders were summarily executed on Mousehold. Kett was captured nearby at the village of Swannington and taken to London for trial. There could be little doubt about the verdict. He was returned to Norwich and spent his last days in the dungeon of the **Guildhall** before being hanged in chains from the battlements of the **Castle** on 7th December; his brother William suffered a similar fate at Wymondham Abbey.

There are still many buildings to be found in the city which were associated with the rebellion, including the **Maid's Head Hotel**, where Lord Sheffield and his men enjoyed their final breakfast, the church of **St Martin at Palace**, where they were soon to be buried, **Bacon House** and **Augustine Steward's** new house in **Tombland**, where the Earl of Warwick was entertained and, of course, the **Guildhall** and **Castle**. Here, near the place where Robert Kett died, is a tablet placed by the citizens of Norwich in 1949 'in reparation and honour to a noble and courageous leader in the struggles of the common people of England to escape from a servile life to the freedom of present conditions.' It is a handsome tribute, if a little late in coming.

The exact location of Dussindale remains undecided but, as the Earl of Warwick's army left the city to give battle via **St Martin's Gate**, it is thought to be to the north of the city, probably between Aylsham Road and Angel Road, around the area of the present-day swimming-pool.

(M)

KETT, ROBERT (1492–1549)

Fourth son of Tom and Margery Kett of Wymondham, some 10 miles south-west of Norwich, he was a tanner by trade but, at the time he led his peasant army on the city in July 1549, he had also become one of the chief landowners in the Wymondham area, owning three manors with a yearly income of £50. The irony is that the root cause of **Kett's Rebellion** was the assault on the livelihood of the small farmers and labourers by landowners intent on depriving them of common land; Kett effectively led a revolt against his own class of prosperous property owners. Indeed, at one stage, he was even to be found joining a group of men to pull down his own fences!

A married man with five sons, Kett was not a young hothead, although modern illustrations tend to portray him as a young man. He was 57 years old at the time of his rebellion – a venerable man by Tudor standards and one who was much respected in his community. He had close connections with Wymondham Abbey and lived near by it. Before its dissolution at the *Reformation*, he had charge of the altar vessels and candles and was a member of a group of Wymondham townsmen who collected money to buy back the bells and lead after the church was despoiled.

Indeed, one of the reasons for Kett's taking up the mantle of leader of the disaffected peasants may well have been the personal enmity which existed between him and John Flowerdew of Hethersett, who desecrated the Abbey and formented trouble by bribing a group of men to pull down Kett's fences.

After the collapse of the rebellion, Robert Kett was suspended from the battlements of Norwich **Castle** and his brother, William, from the west tower of Wymondham Abbey; both trussed up in chains and left to die of starvation and exposure.

The Ketts – variously spelled Cat, Chat, Kette and Knight – were a very old Norfolk family who originally settled in the country around the time of the *Conquest*. Robert and William were not the only members of the family to die for their beliefs. Robert's grandson, Francis Kett M.A., seceded from the established church and was burned for his Unitarian opinions at Wymondham in 1588.

KINGHORN HOUSE

Another of the many fine old houses in Norwich which are in danger of being undiscovered by visitors to the city, this 17th-century building with six distinctive gables stands towards the end of **Pottergate**, just around the corner from **Cow Hill**. The widening of the old Grapes Hill into a dual carriageway, and the disappearance of St Benedicts Plain, has done much to change the character of this area, which has been truncated by the creation of the inner ring road, but Kinghorn House has survived to remind us of an earlier age. It takes it name from Joseph Kinghorn, scholar and divine, minister of St Mary's Baptist Church from 1789 until his death in 1832, who lived here.

KING STREET

The oldest and longest thoroughfare in the city, King Street stretches for nearly a mile from the **Ethelbert Gate** to Bracondale outside the old **city walls**. The Romans may well have passed this way from their town of Venta Icenorum (now Caistor St Edmunds) and it took its earlier name of Conesford Street from Cunegesford, or King's Ford, which almost certainly represents a Danish modification of an earlier Saxon name. From Norman to Stuart times, it was the most important commercial and residential street in the city. Norman ships used the King Street wharves and merchants built their residences and warehouses between the street and the river.

Appropriately, the oldest house in the city – the **Music House** – is situated here. Over the centuries some of England's best-known families had homes in King Street – Pastons, Cokes, Boleyns, Heydons, Howards, Hobarts and Berneys – of which the **Dragon Hall** and **Howard House** are the outstanding survivors.

Before the dissolution of the monasteries, the street boasted a priory, a hospice, two friaries and six churches, in one of which resided **Julian of Norwich**, one of the most celebrated religious figures of her day. Three churches now remain.

While King Street was despoiled after the last war by the construction of a particularly hideous brewery, and even today is threatened by the completion of the inner ring road, it has

Left: St Lawrence the Martyr's 'candle snuffer'.

Below left and right: Spandrel details, St Lawrence the Martyr.

Left: London Street towards National Westminster Bank.

Below: London Street shop fronts and upper windows.

been restored and rebuilt in recent times and much work is still going on to revive its former glories.

Few streets in Norwich reward the patient visitor with so many delightful surprises... but, to see them all, acquire a copy of 'King Street: A guided walk' before setting out.

L

ST LAWRENCE THE MARTYR

A century ago the churchyard gates of St. Lawrence had to be locked at 6.30 pm every Sunday as by that time the church was filled with worshippers. Today this great church in **St Benedict's Street** stands forlorn, empty and locked, awaiting an alternative use. It is a magnificent building, dating from 1472, and one of seven which once stood in this street (it was said that you could hear the bells of 10 churches from a position in St Benedict's Street).

It is best viewed from Westwick Street, where it perches precariously on an 8ft wall, having lost most of its northerly churchyard during road widening. It may be some years before the visitor can see again the interior of the church (which includes a fine hammerbeam roof and a brass to **Sarah Anne Glover**, author of the tonic Sol-fah system) as it is currently in the care of the Norwich Historic Churches Trust, but fortunately the exterior rewards careful study.

The 112ft tower is given a distinctive outline by a spirelet, shaped like a candle-snuffer, over the stair turret, added in 1893 and quite foreign to the area. There are two flights of steps at either end of the church leading from St Benedict's Street to Westwick Street. From St Lawrence Little Steps, beside the base of the tower, look for the carvings in the *spandrels* above the west door. On the left, St Lawrence is shown being broiled to death on a grid-iron at the command of the Roman Emperor Decius; soldiers below replenish the fire while, from the sky, God strikes down the Emperor with a sword (or perhaps a shaft of lightning). The carving on the right portrays the martyrdom of St. Edmund, who stands bristling with arrows. Note, at the bottom right-hand corner, the head of the wolf which guarded the saint's body, peeping from a cave among the bushes. The church was also known as St Lawrence at Quay because the churchyard used to extend down to the riverside.

Under the Revd. Edward Hillyard, this church has associations with **Father Ignatius**, whose 'monks' were allowed to take part in the services.

LAZAR HOUSE

Rescued from demolition in 1902 by the Norwich historian Walter Rye and restored through the architect Owen Bond by Sir Eustace Gurney, this ancient building with its Norman doorway arches and knapped flints was built in the 12th century as a chapel to a leper hospital by **Bishop Herbert de Losinga**. Not unexpectedly, it stood outside the city walls at what is now the corner of Sprowston Road and Gilman Road. Presented to the city in 1921, it became a marvellous setting for Norwich's first branch library, which it remains today.

LIBRARY, CENTRAL

Norwich opened the first public library in England in 1608 and became the first city to adopt the Public Libraries Act of 1850. The modern central library in Bethel Street was designed by the city architect, David Percival, as a reinforced concrete building clad with flint panels. It was opened by the Queen Mother in 1963. The courtyard features a memorial fountain presented by the USAAF 2nd Air Division, which operated from bases in Norfolk and Suffolk during the Second World War.

In addition to the normal book-lending facilities, the central library also houses the American Memorial Library (including the Roll of Honour), the Colman and Rye libraries of local history, the Norfolk and Norwich Law Society's library, the library of the East Anglian Society of Chartered Accountants and the schools' library department.

LIBRARY, SUBSCRIPTION

Designed by Darkins and Blake, the Norfolk and Norwich Subscription Library was built in 1837 on Guildhall Hill on the site of the former Norwich gaol. It ceased to function in 1976 and is now used as an advice centre.

LIDSTER, GEOFFREY (d. 1381)

The Peasants' Revolt was more than a confrontation in London in 1381 between Richard II and his advisers and Wat Tyler's insurgents from Kent and Essex. At the same time, Geoffrey Lidster led an army of rebels to attack Norwich and kill the mayor (they entered the city by swimming across the river on its unprotected eastern flank). The rebels withdrew and, hotly pursued by the 'fighting Bishop' of Norwich, **Henry Despenser**, headed for North Walsham. There the Bishop's army – raised by local landowners who were quick to realize their own interests – defeated them. Ever a man of action, Despenser captured Lidster, condemned him to death, received his last confession, granted him absolution, supervised his execution – and, no doubt, administered the last rites.

LIFE'S GREEN

A curious name for a place of the dead, this is the area in the **Lower Close**, around the east end of the **Cathedral**, which was the burial ground for the monks who inhabited the Benedictine monastery for more than four centuries. It is notable today for the grave of **Edith Cavell**.

LIND, JENNY (1820–1887)

Known as the Swedish nightingale, this great singer gave two concerts in Norwich in 1849 and donated the proceeds – £1,253, equivalent now to well over £30,000 – to establish the Jenny Lind children's hospital. The money was used to buy a row of houses in **Pottergate** which were converted into a hospital with 12 beds. Jenny visited the new infirmary and wrote afterwards: 'Of all the money God allowed me to give away when my poor throat could call an audience to listen to its production, none has borne a nobler fruit than the Jenny Lind Hospital in Norwich.' The city's associations with this 19th-century superstar continue today through the Jenny Lind children's department at the **Norfolk and Norwich Hospital**.

LITTLE PORTION MEETING HOUSE

Situated in Cross Lane, this was formerly the **Rifleman Ale House**, the local tavern of Norwich's most famous artist, **John Crome**, and later the home of the **Dirty Shirt Club**.

LOLLARDS PIT

Lollards were followers of John Wycliffe (?1324–1384), a priest who had the temerity to write for the common people in English rather than Latin and to declare that the clergy should be poor, as Christ was. This made him very unpopular with the church authorities and, after his death, he was declared a heretic and his followers – there were many in East Anglia – were persecuted. The Lollards Pit was where they were burned to death.

A green plaque on the **Bridge House** public house opposite **Bishop Bridge** claims this to be the site of the pit but a much older memorial – now vanished – placed it more reliably to the right at a spot now occupied by the car park of a DIY store.

The pit had been formed when clay was dug from the hillside, possibly during the construction of the **Cathedral**. The resulting hollow saw many hundreds of people suffer an agonising death in the 15th and 16th centuries, the most famous of whom was the Protestant martyr **Thomas Bilney**. They would usually be held in the dungeons of the **Guildhall** and then taken in procession through the city and over Bishop Bridge. Such a sight must have acted as a powerful stimulant to retain the orthodox faith of the day but this did not prevent many Norfolk people, years after the last of Wycliffe's followers had died, from choosing the path of martyrdom.

The word Lollard, by the way, comes from the Low German/Dutch word lollen (to sing) and was originally applied to a religious sect formed in Antwerp in 1300 for the care of the sick and burial of the dead. Members of the sect sang dirges at funerals and were eventually declared heretics by the religious authorities.

LONDON STREET

A busy shopping street since the 19th century, between **Gentleman's Walk** and Bank Plain, this was the second street of its kind in the country to be turned into a traffic-free area in the 1960s. In medieval times it was known as Cockey Street from the small stream, or cockey, which ran through it and is believed still to run under it.

Among the many fine shops are two interesting memorials – a plaque outside the former restaurant of **Louis Marchesi**, founder of the international Round Table movement, and at the corner of Opie Street a stone marking the spot where a sedan chair plied for hire in the 18th century.

DE LOSINGA, BISHOP HERBERT

(? 1045–1119)

There is evidence to suggest that the founder of Norwich **Cathedral** was an Anglo-Norman, born in Suffolk (perhaps at Hoxne) and educated at the Abbey of Fécamp. He was appointed Abbot of Ramsey Abbey in 1087 and then, four years later, Bishop of Thetford by William II, at the same time that his father was made an Abbot of Winchester. It was said that de Losinga committed the crime of simony – that is, paying a large sum of money for these two appointments – and certainly much penitence was expressed, including resigning his post and going to Rome for an interview with the Pope, who reappointed him. Suggestions that de Losinga founded the Cathedral as an act of penance can be discounted. It is more likely that, as Norwich became the centre of civic administration and trade in East Anglia, 30 years after the arrival of the **Normans**, he felt this was the place to construct a new Norman cathedral to complement the **Castle**.

Thus de Losinga became the last Bishop of Thetford and the first Bishop of Norwich, moving to the city in 1094 and beginning the building of the Cathedral two years later.

A man of great energy, like all the leading Anglo-Normans, he was also responsible for establishing St Leonard's Priory on the edge of **Mousehold Heath**, St Nicholas's Church in Great Yarmouth, St Margaret's in King's Lynn and a hospital in honour of St Paul. He was also an important figure at court and a friend of Henry I's Queen, Matilda.

He lived to a great age and saw his cathedral dedicated in 1101. It had been built as far as the *nave* by the time of his death on 22nd July 1119. He is buried in front of the high altar. He left behind 14 sermons and 60 letters, in one of which he commented: 'From God alone

Above: Lower Goat Lane.

Below: Maddermarket Theatre.

I expect a recompense for all the good things I may have done in Norwich.' It seems a fitting epitaph.

LOWER CLOSE

Almost entirely residential part of the Norwich **Cathedral** close, which is the largest of its kind in the country. It comprises some excellent houses, converting or replacing the old priory buildings after the *Reformation.* The road to the river (culminating in the water-gate or **Pull's Ferry**) marks the course of the canal dug to bring building materials to the cathedral site. Lower Close is also the site of **Life's Green** at the eastern end of the cathedral, the grave of **Edith Cavell** and the remains of the Priory's infirmary and refectory. **Upper Close** is described under a separate entry.

LOWER GOAT LANE

This narrow thoroughfare joining Guildhall Hill and **Pottergate** dates back at least to the 13th century and was formerly known as Stonegate, probably because a market for stoneware was located there. It takes its present name from two pubs which used to stand in the street – the New Goat and the Old Goat. The Old Goat was kept by Charles Goat and the New Goat by Eliza Mountain! Upper Goat Lane, which has associations with Elizabeth Fry and the old Quaker Meeting House, runs parallel to it.

LYHART, BISHOP WALTER (d. 1472)

Responsible for the magnificent lierne vaulting and carved bosses in the *nave* of the **Cathedral,** he marked his work with a *rebus* (a hart lying in water) and his coat of arms (a shield with a bull upon it) carved on *corbels* at the top of each alternative pillar.

The same motifs can be seen in the *spandrels* of the central arch of the organ screen, for which Lyhart was also responsible. The great west window was also constructed under Lyhart using money left by his predecessor, Bishop Alnwick, who had earlier built the **Alnwick** or Bishop's Palace Gate.

~M~

(M)

MACE, JEM (1831–1910)

Norfolk has produced many famous boxers, one of the earliest of whom was born at Beeston, near Dereham, the son of a blacksmith, and went on to become champion prize fighter of the world. One of Jem's earliest fights was with another Norfolk man, John 'Licker' Pratt, later landlord of the **Hampshire Hog**. It was a bare-knuckle encounter at Drayton and lasted two hours before the 19-year-old Mace was defeated.

Like so many prize fighters, Jem took a pub – the Swan on Swan Lane, now demolished – where, one imagines, the customers tended not to give him much aggravation. He first won the British championship in 1862 (after 43 rounds), lost it in a return bout, claimed it again when the new champion retired and held it for seven years.

The pinnacle of his career came in 1870 when he defeated Tom Allen of the United States for the world title. He lectured and gave exhibition bouts into his seventies and is buried in Anfield Cemetery, Liverpool.

MACKINTOSH, JOHN & SONS LTD.

Now part of Rowntree Mackintosh, which in turn was acquired by the Nestlé group, this great chocolate-making plant behind the remains of the **city walls** in Chapelfield Road owes its origins to a Norwich chemist, A. J. Caley, who began to manufacture mineral waters in his cellar in 1860. His business prospered and, to balance seasonal demands, he began the production of cocoa, chocolate and Christmas crackers in the 1880s. Caleys became part of Mackintosh's in 1932.

MADDERMARKET

The area where red vegetable dye prepared from the madder root was sold to city weavers. Chiefly notable now for **St John's Church** and the **Maddermarket Theatre**.

MADDERMARKET THEATRE

Inspired by the late **Nugent Monck**, this world-renowned home of the Norwich Players was opened in September 1921 in a building which was formerly a Roman Catholic chapel, a baking powder factory and a Salvation Army citadel. Monck built a replica of a Shakespearian theatre within at a cost of £3,300 raised from supporters. Today productions range from old time music hall to Christmas pantomime and includes all the best of classical and modern drama. The actors are amateur and anonymous, with a professional director. The Maddermarket offers an excellent counterbalance to the professional **Theatre Royal**.

MAGDALEN GATE

Also known as the leper's gate from the **Lazar House** which stood outside it, this was the last of the city's gates to be fortified, in around 1339. It was repaired in 1756, whitewashed in 1783 and was the last gate to be demolished in 1808. It stood at what is now the junction of **Magdalen Street** and Magpie Road.

MAGDALEN STREET

Travellers approaching from the north in medieval times would have entered the city through the **Magdalen Gate** and thus along Magdalen Street, across **Fye Bridge** and into **Tombland**. The whole character of the street changed in the late 1960s with the construction of a flyover to take the new inner ring road and the development of Anglia Square shopping precinct to the west, dominated by Sovereign House, the headquarters of the Stationery Office.

It remains a busy thoroughfare and shopping street with some interesting buildings, the best of which are Sackville Place and **Gurney Court**. It has three pre-Reformation churches – **St Simon and St Jude, St Clement** and **St Saviour**, the latter two having associations with **Matthew Parker**, the only Norwich priest to reach the pinnacle of his profession as Archbishop of Canterbury.

MAID'S HEAD HOTEL

'I praye yow make hym goode cheer...if I shall be sent for, and he tary at Norwich there whylst it were best to settle his horse at the Maydes Hedde, and I shall be content for their expences.'

When **John Paston** wrote those words on 2nd November 1472 to announce the arrival of a visitor, the Maid's Head had already been in existence for more than 200 years. Today it challenges any hotel in Britain to prove a longer record of continuous service – more than 700 years – but no credible contender has yet appeared.

Francis Blomefield suggested that the hotel stands on the site of a palace belonging to the early Norman bishops, while later it was surmised that the various **friary** orders in the city used the palace as an inn for the accommodation of pilgrims.

An inscription on the doors to the old coaching yard facing Wensum Street tells us that Queen Elizabeth I stayed at the inn during her visit to the city in 1578. Don't believe a word of it – the Queen spent her nights during the week-long visit at the old **Bishop's Palace** in the cathedral grounds.

The exterior of the Maid's Head looks too modern for such antiquity but inside can be found Norman, Tudor, Jacobean and Georgian work. The first regular stage-coach to London, the Norwich Machine, set out from here in 1762 (a bone-shaking 15-hour journey at a cost of one guinea) and continued until 1856, when the dominance of the railways ended for all time the so-called romance of the great stage routes.

MARCHESI, LOUIS (1898–1968)

Restaurateur from **London Street** who founded the Round Table, an association of young business and professional men which is now an international movement, at a meeting in **Stuart Hall** (now Cinema City) on 14th March 1927. There is a pub named after him opposite the **Erpingham Gate** in **Tombland**.

ST MARGARET

One of the three remaining medieval churches in **St Benedict Street** – once there were seven, all of which are now redundant – St Margaret has found a new use as a gymnasium. It has a large churchyard, a typically Norwich flint tower with buttresses which end at the belfry stage, and porches to the north and south, one with a single storey and the other with two. The south porch has stone benches on either side, from which the destitute of the parish would be removed before services began. The interior was much repaired and restored in the last century.

MARKET PLACE

Part of the New Burgh, or French Borough, which the Domesday Book tells us was created by Earl Ralf, who was made Earl of East Anglia shortly after the *Conquest*, a market has stood on this spot for over 900 years. The original toll house, used for the collection of market tolls, stood on the site of the **Guildhall** – indeed, its undercroft forms the crypt below the east end of the building – and until the introduction of shops in the 17th century all retail selling took place here or in subsidiary markets in side streets.

Today the market place is one of the city's best known and most attractive features. It is the home of the provisions market, comprising 200 stalls characterized by brightly coloured canvas covers (known as tilts), and is open six days a week. It fronts on to **Gentleman's Walk**, which was closed to traffic and turned into a pedestrian area in 1988, thus adding even more to the market's appeal.

ST MARTIN IN BALLIVA

The vanished church of Norwich **Castle**, St Martin took its curious name from the fact that it was within the Castle's bailiwick, or area of jurisdiction. All who died within the Castle were buried here until 1562, when the church was demolished and its function transferred to **St Michael at Thorn**. There is a green plaque marking the original site of the church on the wall of the steps leading to **Prospect House**, the head office of Eastern Counties Newspapers. The site of St Michael at Thorn – another church of which no trace remains – is also on land occupied by ECN.

ST MARTIN'S GATE

Situated in Oak Street, and demolished at the end of the 18th century, this was probably the gate through which the **Earl of Warwick** led his men to crush the peasant army outside the city walls and conclude **Kett's Rebellion** in 1549. The area of the site was also known as Fuller's Hole after Henry Fuller, sheriff in 1528 and mayor in 1544, who had a house here.

ST MARTIN AT OAK

One of the city's most out-of-the-way churches, it takes its name from an oak tree

Left: St Michael Coslany (St Miles).

Below: St Michael at Plea's clock.

which once stood in the churchyard, displaying in its branches a figure of the Virgin that was much venerated in the 15th century. The church is now used as a night shelter.

ST MARTIN AT PALACE

In many ways a typical example of a Norwich medieval church – a western tower, a nave that is taller than the chancel, and a two-storeyed porch on the south – St Martin is unique in having *clerestory* windows in the shape of quatrefoils, or four-leaf clovers. It is a pleasant little church, standing opposite the **Alnwick Gate** and notable for other unusual features, including Anglo-Saxon 'long and short' stonework at the east end – relics, perhaps, of an earlier church on this site – and a fine east window, with three stained-glass figures, which was the work of the firm of William Morris, the notable Victorian poet, artist and designer.

Inside is a large monument to Lady Elizabeth Calthorpe (1578), whose family took over the nearby Erpingham House from the descendants of **Sir Thomas Erpingham**. Here also are buried Lord Sheffield and 35 of his followers who were killed outside during one of the fiercest battles of **Kett's Rebellion**, although there is no remaining monument to them. Sadly for such an attractive church, St Martin is now redundant; it is currently being used by the probation service.

MARTINEAU, HARRIET (1802–1876)

Writer of novels, children's stories, and books on travel, history and economics, and an important member of the rationalist movement during the 19th century – a 'new woman', indeed – she was born in the same house in **Gurney Court** as **Elizabeth Fry**.

ST MARY COSLANY

The round tower of this little church just off Duke Street is the oldest standing structure in the city, dating from 1070, nearly 30 years before the **Cathedral** was even started. It has excellent double belfry openings, with V-shaped heads and recessed shafts, and the main body of the church was built against it in 1477. The south porch is a delight, as is the fine arch-braced roof. The whole church follows a cruciform shape with nave, chancel and *transepts* but no aisles.

St Mary Coslany has strong associations with the **Norwich School of Painting. John Sell Cotman** was baptised here in 1782 and, a decade later, **John Crome** married Phoebe Berney. This was also the baptismal church of **Luke Hansard**, who gave his name to the journals of the House of Commons.

There are handsome stained-glass windows bearing the coats of arms of the Springfield family (silk merchants who provided mayors in 1829, 1836 and 1863) and Peter Finch, a brewer who was mayor in 1827. St Mary is now open every day as a craft and design centre.

ST MARY IN THE FIELDS

Medieval religious college – closed in 1544 – on the site of the present-day **Assembly House** and **Noverre Cinema**; some of the original timbers remain behind the Georgian façade. The name lives on in Chapelfield Road and **Chapelfield** Gardens, which was originally an open space belonging to the priests. The church of the college was reputed to be even larger than **St Peter Mancroft**.

ST MARY THE LESS

This is the hidden church of Norwich, with an entrance in Queens Street but otherwise concealed completely from view. It has been like this for a long time, for **Francis Blomefield** described it as having 'houses built in the west, south and east end of the churchyard, and in the north part is a stonecutter's yard'.

As the church nearest to the **Ethelbert Gate**, it was known in medieval times as St Mary at the Monastery Gate and then became St Mary the Less to distinguish it from **St Mary Coslany**.

A more familiar name to many Norwich people is 'the French church', for it became the place of worship of the French Protestant **strangers** in 1637. Earlier – in 1564 – it was used as a cloth hall in which the newly arrived Dutch and Walloon weavers sold their materials.

A small church, it is one of the oldest in the city, probably dating from the 13th century. It has served a remarkable number of purposes during its history; after nearly two centuries as a place of worship for the French, it was leased to the Swedenborgians and then became a non-conformist Catholic Apostolic Church. It fell into disuse in 1953, became a furniture store and was then restored in 1988 and offered for sale by the trustees of the French Church Charity. Appropriately enough, the proceeds of the sale were distributed by the trust in the form of grants to help educate and train young Norwich people descended from French protestants. Plans were announced in 1989 to convert the premises into a Dutch and Flemish museum and study centre.

ST MARY IN THE MARSH

This ancient parish church in the **Lower Close** of the **Cathedral** was destroyed in 1570 and the parishioners were given the use of St Luke's Chapel in its place. A parochial service is held there every month. One remaining wall of the old church remains inside Nos. 10 and 11 in the Lower Close.

ST MICHAEL COSLANY

Perhaps the most striking church in a city packed with churches, St Michael (also known as St Miles) has many aspects but it is best to start with the glorious display of *flushwork* upon the south aisle and much of the chancel. These intricate patterns of flint and freestone were likened in 1842 to 'The inlaid ivory work of old cabinets.' The flushwork of the aisle and chapel is 15th century while that of the south and east walls of the chancel is a remarkably skilful copy, the result of restoration in 1883/84.

The church is impressive from all angles, particularly the tall west tower, the *nave* (without *clerestory* windows) buttressed by broad aisles lit by great wide windows, and a lovely entrance door. Like its companion, **St Mary Coslany**, it is now redundant, being used as a sports hall.

ST MICHAEL AT PLEA

So called because the medieval church plea courts were held within, St Michael is mostly built of flint, while the fine two-storey porch is of light ashlar stone; in *spandrels* over the entrance are reliefs of St Michael and the dragon.

The tower is particularly striking, despite four clumsy pinnacles added by the Victorians, who could never see anything plain and fine without wanting to decorate it. A more attractive feature from the last century, however, is the clock, dated 1827, with its inscription familiar to generations of Norwich people – 'Forget me not'. The city has not forgotten this attractive building at the junction of Bank Plain and Queen Street for, after many years of neglect, it has been restored and is used as an antique market and Sue Ryder coffee shop.

ST MICHAEL AT THORN

Apart from a green plaque, no trace now remains of this pre-*Conquest* church at the junction of **Ber Street** and Thorn Lane. Many of those who died at the **Castle** were buried here. The church was bombed out of existence in 1942. A fine Norman archway survived, however, and it is now to be found in the rebuilt church of **St Julian**.

Below: Mustard Shop sign.

Above: Mischief Tavern sign.

MISCHIEF TAVERN

Standing close to **Fye Bridge**, this popular pub is notable for its inn sign and its antiquity. A stone fireplace inside dated 1599 bears the mark of a mason now at rest in the churchyard of **St Clement** next door, but the building itself dates back to 1312. The sign is based on an 18th-century cartoon of a man loaded down with the cares of life, including his drunken wife, a monkey and a jackdaw. The full name of the pub is The Man with a Load of Mischief on his Back and the original cartoon was painted by William Hogarth. There was only one other pub so called (in London) and it is believed that the sign was copied by one of the **Norwich School** of painters, perhaps **John Crome** himself.

MONCK, NUGENT (1878–1958)

Born in Shropshire, he learned to act at Liverpool Academy and paid his first visit to Norwich to produce a pageant. Such was his reception that he decided to stay and, in 1911, gathered together 'a few friends to read and talk over plays that interested them, which we were certain were not the plays the public supported.' From there it was a natural step to begin acting the plays, initially at the **Music House** in **King Street**. After the First World War, Monck found a permanent home for his theatre in the Maddermarket area, building a replica of an Elizabethan theatre within a former Roman Catholic chapel. Thus, in 1921, the **Maddermarket Theatre** came into existence.

For 40 years he lived in a house in Ninham's Court, off Chapelfield North. He was, by all accounts, a remarkable man, much missed by all his friends upon his death; without his tremendous contribution to the theatre, Norwich would be a poorer place.

MONKS

The majority of the city's medieval religious foundations were **friaries**, with the notable exception of the community of Benedictine monks who had charge of the **Cathedral** from its earliest days until the *Reformation*. The Bishop was their official head but day-to-day responsibility for the 60 monks and the monastery rested with the Prior. When in 1538 Henry VIII ordered the dissolution of the monasteries, the monks became canons, petty canons and singing men, headed by a Dean, and the Cathedral passed into the care of a group of clergy called the Chapter.

MORSE, JOHN

See **St Catherine's Close**.

MOUNTERGATE

A corruption of the word Parmentergate or Parmountergate – the place of the leather workers – this road runs between **King Street** and Rose Lane. At one time it was called St Faith's Lane; the name is perpetuated in an ancient winding street to the north of Prince of Wales Road which was the site of the old Horse Fair and which leads, almost by stealth, to the **Ethelbert Gate** to the **Cathedral**.

MOUSEHOLD HEATH

In medieval times the heath stretched as far as Salhouse Broad. It was enclosed in 1801 at a time when much of it belonged to the Dean and Chapter of the **Cathedral**. In 1880 the Anglican church conveyed it to the Corporation on condition that it was used for the recreation of the people of Norwich for ever.

Today, Mousehold Heath comprises 184 acres of undulating heathland to the north-east which is one of the city's continuing joys for naturalists, sports enthusiasts and walkers alike. There is an excellent view of the city from the Mottram memorial on **St James Hill**.

The heath gained its curious name in late-

Saxon times – the meaning may be Mouse Wood, from the large number of mice that were found there, or perhaps it was a derogatory term to indicate that the ground was too poor to produce enough for anything more than a mouse to live off. Certainly the heath's mix of brick-earth, gravel and Norwich crag has never encouraged cultivation.

MUSEUMS

Norwich has six museums of various sizes and degrees of importance. Some are described in more detail under separate entries.

Bridewell:

Museum of local industries and rural crafts, situated since 1925 in a 14th-century merchant's house in Bridewell Alley. Open: Mon – Sat 10 a.m. to 5 p.m.

Castle:

One of the oldest buildings in Norwich, the Castle keep houses museums of art (especially the Norwich School of Painting), local archeology, social history and natural history in former prison buildings and a rotunda, built in 1969, which occupies the former exercise yard. There is a magnificent view of the city from the battlements. Open: Mon – Sat 10 a.m. to 5 p.m., Sun 2 p.m. to 5 p.m.

Church:

The redundant church of **St Peter Hungate** in **Princes Street** has been a civic museum of church art and craftsmanship since 1936. A variety of objects are displayed, including rare medieval vestments and illuminated manuscript service books, English alabaster carvings, Russian icons, Communion plate, musical instruments and many others. The most unusual exhibit, perhaps, is a 14th-century coffin with a skeleton in it, found on the site of the **Carmelite Friary**. It is believed to be the remains of a woman, indicating that she was a benefactress of the friary, who was prepared to pay for the privilege of being buried in the friary precincts. Open: Mon – Sat 10 a.m. to 5 p.m.

Regimental:

Situated in the Victorian **Shire Hall** next to the **Castle**, the Royal Norfolk Regimental Museum contains exhibits of all kinds commemorating the Royal Norfolk Regiment which – under various titles – has had a continuous existence since 1685 and now forms part of the Royal Anglians. Open: Mon – Sat 10a.m. to 5p.m., Sun. 2p.m. to 5p.m.

Strangers Hall, museum of domestic life:

Medieval town mansion built around two courtyards and fronting **Charing Cross**, with the south side overlooking a garden and the east end of **St Gregory's Church**.

It is a complex, rambling building in which there are 23 rooms open to the public, most of them furnished in period style, from the early 16th to the late 19th centuries. There is an extraordinarily wide range of exhibits, from a dolls' house dated 1700 to the Lord Mayor's coach. The Great Hall is particularly fine and features a crown-post roof which dates from 1539.

Strangers Hall was presented to the city in 1922 by the noted Norwich antiquary Leonard Bolingbroke (1859–1927), who had established a private museum in the house. The origin of the name is unknown. It may refer to the refugees, or **'strangers'**, from Holland who settled here in the reign of Elizabeth I (some of whom are believed to have lived in the house); or to the priests and monks who fled from revolutionary France at the end of the 19th century and are said to have lodged here with a Roman Catholic priest whose chapel is now the **Maddermarket Theatre**. Open: Mon – Sat 10 a.m. to 5 p.m.

Telephone Museum:

The smallest museum in the city, situated in one of the smallest houses, it is contained in a remaining fragment of a Tudor merchant's home in St Andrew's Street. All that remains of the city mansion of Francis Rugge, MP for Norwich and mayor between 1587 and 1602, is the entrance and first floor. Since 1970 this timber-framed survivor, with herring-bone brickwork, diamond-leaded windows, carved over-lintels and an oak doorway arch, has housed the Norwich Telephone Area Museum. Worth a visit – if you are interested in telephones. British Telecom will arrange a visit for you. Telephone Norwich 661714.

MUSIC HOUSE

The oldest house in the city is found, appropriately, in one of its oldest thoroughfares, **King Street**. When it was completed in 1175 it was only the third stone building in the city, the others being the **Cathedral** and **Castle**. It was built by a Jewish merchant and moneylender, named **Jurnet**. Being in a high-risk business – financially and racially – he built a strong, easily defended house well away from the centre of the city, with an undercroft, which still exists, to store his riches.

It passed into the hands of some of Norfolk's greatest families, including the **Pastons** in 1488 and Sir Edward Coke, Recorder of Norwich and Lord Chief Justice of England in the 17th century. It takes its name from the City Waits, a band of five minstrels who were the official Norwich musicians. Each lived in King Street and successive generations of them practised in this house from their formation in the reign of Elizabeth I until they were paid off by the city in 1790.

The Music House came into the possession of Youngs Crawshay & Youngs brewery who presented it, together with neighbouring **Wensum Lodge**, to the Norfolk Education Committee. The whole complex is now an adult education centre. The name of the founder is preserved within the original undercroft in the form of a bar called Jurnet's.

MUSTARD SHOP AND MUSEUM

Colman's reconstruction of a Victorian shop in **Bridewell Alley** sells more varieties of mustard than you ever thought existed, plus ancilliary kitchen-ware to go with it. Well worth a visit for an unusual souvenir of the city. It was opened in 1973 to commemorate the 150th anniversary of the partnership between Jeremiah Colman and his nephew, James, to form the mustard firm of J. J. Colman. See also **Colmans of Norwich**. Open: Mon, Wed, Thurs, Fri, Sat 9 a.m. to 5.30 p.m.; Tues. 9.30 a.m. to 5.30 p.m.

N

NATIONAL WESTMINSTER BANK

There is no late 17th-century English Baroque architecture in Norwich but Palmer and Holden's excellent 1924 pastiche of Wren, the National Westminster Bank in **London Street**, gets pretty close. It was created 'to provide the ancient city with a building that should not fail the traditions of its splendid heritage'.

NEDEHAM GATE

Also known as St Stephen's Gate, this was

the principal approach to the city from the south. It was a handsome gateway, as befitted the entrance to the city for travellers from London, with two battlemented towers – round at the front, square at the back – and the city arms carved in stone over the door.

The gateway was demolished in 1793 but there is an excellent mural by Moray-Smith on the wall of the Coachmaker's Arms in nearby St. Stephen's Road, depicting it as it would have looked in the 17th century.

NEEDHAM

Probably the largest of the 8th or 9th century settlements which eventually formed Norwich, it vanished beneath the **Castle** when the **Normans** arrived in 1067. In its prime it probably stretched east to **King Street** and west to **Westlegate**. An 11th-century church found during excavations at the rear of the Agricultural Hall early in the 1980s almost certainly formed part of it. Further excavations in the area have since been carried out by the Norfolk Archeological Unit prior to the construction of **Castle Mall**.

NELSON, HORATIO (1758–1805)

The statue of the Norfolk hero which stands on the grassed area in the **Upper Close** of the **Cathedral** looks upon a scene that would have been familiar to the young Horatio when he was a pupil at the **Edward VI School** in the 1760s. The son of the rector of Burnham Thorpe in north Norfolk, he received his brief education (on land at least) here and at the Paston School, North Walsham, from which he was removed at the tender age of 12 to join the Royal Navy.

While at school in the city, he is thought to have lodged in **Tombland Alley** opposite the **Erpingham Gate** but it is also possible that he lived in **Suckling House** in St Andrew's Street, for he was related through his late mother to the Suckling family, which in turn gave him connections with the mighty Walpoles, the Norfolk family that had provided Britain's first Prime Minister some 50 years earlier.

Nelson saw little of the city after leaving it for North Walsham and glory as one of Britain's greatest sea heroes. Apart from the statue – which was originally sited in the **market place**, next to that of the **Duke of Wellington**, and moved to its present position in 1856 – the most enduring memento of the city's foremost fighting man is a Spanish admiral's sword kept in the regalia room at the **Guildhall**. Nelson took it from the Admiral, who had been killed in the battle of St Vincent, and sent it to the Mayor of Norwich on 26th February 1797 with a covering letter, which is also on display. It is in the handwriting learned and formed in his native Norfolk; a few months later he had to learn to write again, for he lost his right arm in July of that year.

NELSON, HOTEL

Stands on the site of the original foundry which gave its name to **Foundry Bridge**; its forerunner was the Great Eastern Hotel built opposite **Thorpe Station** to accommodate Victorian rail travellers. When it was opened in 1971 by Sir Mark Henig, Chairman of the English Tourist Board, it was the first new hotel to be built in the city for 100 years.

NINHAM COURT

Passage leading from Chapelfield North to Bethel Street named after the artist **Henry Ninham**, whose house stands at the Chapelfield end. It was formerly called Masters Court.

Ⓜ

NINHAM, HENRY (1793–1874)

While not an artist of the first rank, he has

Above: Norwich Union buildings – old and new.

Left: Statue, Norwich Union head office.

left us a fascinating insight into the city as he knew it through his etchings of what he called the picturesque antiquities of Norwich, many of which are no more. He also specialized in coats of arms which were displayed in the coaches of wealthy citizens.

NORFOLK AND NORWICH HOSPITAL

See **Hospital.**

NORMANS

More than any other people, the Norman-French shaped the city as we know it today. From their arrival a year after the conquest of England by the man who was to become King William I, nothing was ever the same again. In an explosion of building these energetic entrepreneurs created a Norman zone across the city, the most important elements of which still dominate today – the **Castle**, the **Cathedral** and the **market place**. This provided a new focus around which the Anglo-Norman borough developed. By the time Norwich had recovered from the shock caused by the arrival of a small garrison of professional fighting men to dominate a population of some 5,000 people and the sweeping away of so much that was familiar to them, the city had acquired a new importance as a cathedral town and a military and administrative centre.

NORTHAMPTON, MARQUIS OF
(1513–1571)

Commander of an expeditionary force sent by the Protector Somerset to eject **Robert Kett** and his rebels from the city in 1549. His army was defeated in the battle of St. Martin's Plain and he vanished into historical obscurity. See **Kett's Rebellion**.

NORTHWICK

Middle Saxon settlement thought to be in the general area of **Magdalen Street/St George's Street**. By 920 it had developed into a fortified administrative and market centre with its own mint. The mint made Northwick a burgh and this, together with the fact that it controlled three important river crossings – at **Bishop Bridge, Whitefriars Bridge** and **Fye Bridge** – meant that Northwick became the dominant settlement in the later Saxon town, with its great market and the palace of the Earl of East Anglia both situated in **Tombland**.

A coin from the time of Aethelstan of England, minted in the burgh between 920 and 940, gives us the earliest written record of the name Norwich, expressed as NORWIC.

NORWICH CITY FOOTBALL CLUB

Called the Canaries from their yellow and green strip (the city was once famous for breeding these exotic birds), the club was officially formed in June 1902 but it is on record that a Norwich Football Club played at Newmarket Road as early as 1868. Norwich City F.C., too, had their first ground at Newmarket Road, moving later to the Nest in Rosary Road (now the site of an industrial estate – but you can still see the old terraces) and then to its present ground in Carrow Road in 1935. Over the years the club has progressed from the Norfolk and Suffolk League to the first division of the English Football League, which it led for a number of months during the 1988/89 season. Collectors of obscure facts might be interested to know that the Carrow Road pitch is just two metres above sea level, making it the lowest in the Football League.

NORWICH SCHOOL

See **Edward VI School.**

NORWICH SCHOOL OF PAINTING

Norwich is the only city in England to be able

to claim its own historical 'school' of painting, similar in many respects to the local schools of 17th-century Holland.

The term 'Norwich School' is comparatively recent. When the school was founded in 1803 it was known as the Norwich Society; it came into existence 'for the purpose of an enquiry into the rise, progress and present state of painting, architecture and sculpture, with a view to pointing out the best methods of study to attain the greater perfection of these arts'. **John Crome** and Robert Ladbrooke began it all and eventually more than 30 artists met in taverns to discuss their work and plan exhibitions.

What particularly distinguishes these artists is their devotion to their own locality and their contribution to the naturalism developed by the greatest of all East Anglian painters, John Constable. The best-known of the Norwich School of painters are John Crome, **John Sell Cotman**, George Vincent and **Joseph Stannard**. Examples of the works of these painters, and many of their associates, may be seen in the Colman galleries at the **Castle** Museum.

NORWICH UNION INSURANCE GROUP

Thomas Bignold established himself in the city in 1783 as a wine merchant and banker. He founded in quick succession the Norwich General Assurance Office, the Norwich Union Fire Insurance Society and the Norwich Union Life Insurance Society. All did well from the start, despite considerable competition, laying the foundations for the modern insurance giant which is the city's major employer and controls branch offices throughout the United Kingdom and in many countries overseas.

Its head office in Surrey Street – a magnificent building designed by **George Skipper** – is known as the marble hall. Skipper discovered a quantity of marble destined for Westminster Cathedral which arrived too late to be used. He persuaded his clients to buy it and created with it a superb marble hall and boardroom. The architectural historian Sir Nikolaus Pevsner described it as 'one of the most convinced Edwardian buildings in the country'.

NOVERRE CINEMA

A 17th-century town house once owned by the Hobarts of Blickling Hall which now forms the right-hand wing of the **Assembly House**. It takes its name from Frank Noverre, a Victorian dancing master, who had his dancing academy within it and organized an annual ball in the Assembly House.

~O~

Ⓜ

OBELISK FOUNTAIN

A drinking fountain erected in the shape of an obelisk by John Harvey Gurney in 1860 in **Tombland** to commemorate the machinery which stood on this spot between 1700 and 1850 which was used to raise and store water for the higher parts of the city.

OCTAGON CHAPEL

Thomas Ivory's masterpiece in Colegate, variously described as the non-conformist cathedral by its supporters and the devil's cucumber frame by those of a more conventional religious nature. It was built in 1756 for the Presbyterians but later became a place of

Above: Octagon Chapel.

Right: Amelia Opie's sta

Below: Old Meeting House.

worship for the Unitarians. In the 18th century it was the intellectual powerhouse of the city, filled with wealthy and highly literate dissenters, many of whom made a permanent mark on their society. They included James and **Harriet Martineau**, John and **Amelia Opie**, the Aldersons, the Norgates, the Taylors and the Bolingbrokes.

It is a magnificent building although a little too ornate, perhaps, for the austere tastes of the great John Wesley, who visited it in 1787 and wondered afterwards 'how it could be thought the old coarse gospel would find admission here.'

Actually Thomas Ivory – who was much involved with the building of the **Assembly House** at the time – acquired the striking octagonal design from another architect. He chanced to come across a rejected plan by James Gibbs for a circular church in St Martin in the Fields, London, and skilfully adapted it as his submission to a committee set up by the Presbyterian Church to find a suitable design.

OLD MEETING HOUSE

It takes something of a search to find this, the oldest and one of the finest of the non-conformist meeting houses in the country. It stands at the end of an alley opposite **St Clement's Church** in **Colegate** and next door to that other monument to non-conformism, the **Octagon Chapel**. When the Old Meeting House was built in 1693, it was a wise precaution for the Congregationalist Church to keep what today would be described as a low profile – it was, after all, less than 60 years since the **Revd. William Bridge** had been forced to flee from Norwich to Holland because of his Independent views. Hence the Old Meeting House was tucked away out of sight to avoid drawing attention to itself; by the time the Octagon Chapel was constructed in the mid-18th century, however, the non-conformists were sufficiently self-confident to place it where it could hardly be overlooked.

The Old Meeting House has an attractive little forecourt and a gracious symmetrical façade of red brick, divided into five bays with tall pilasters with Corinthian columns of Portland stone. The interior is lit by two rows of sash windows, said to be the first of their kind to be installed in the city.

(M)

OPIE, AMELIA (1769–1853)

The only child of John Alderson, a prominent Norwich physician, she married the portrait painter John Opie in 1798, moved to London and became a fashionable writer. Widowed in 1807, she returned to Norwich to live with her father in **Colegate**, becoming a Quaker and an intimate of the **Gurney** family. She was closely associated with a group of writers and thinkers who did much to shape new attitudes in the early 19th century and is commemorated today by Opie Street, off Castle Meadow, where she lived in her old age.

ORFORD HILL

Formerly known as Hog Hill – presumably because it led to the old swine market near **All Saints** – this short stretch of road off Red Lion Street was renamed in honour of **George Walpole**, the eccentric 3rd Earl of Orford, who gave generously to a public subscription to improve the area in the 18th century.

P

Ⓜ

PARKER, MATTHEW (1504–1573)

The only Norwich-born cleric to reach the top of his profession as Archbishop of Canterbury, he came to the notice of Henry VIII while at Corpus Christi College, Cambridge, and was made chaplain to the ill-fated Anne Boleyn, the second of the King's six wives. On the eve of her execution, she placed her baby daughter in his charge. The baby grew up to become Elizabeth I, who made Parker Archbishop of Canterbury in 1559, the year after she ascended the throne.

In 1549 he was Master of Corpus Christi and happened to be in Norwich with his family during **Kett's Rebellion**. He showed great courage in preaching to the rebels in their camp but his appeals to them to lay down their arms and return home met with a hostile response and he was compelled to make a hasty retreat from **Mousehold Heath** and later from the city.

An incurably inquisitive man, interested in everybody's business, the Archbishop was nicknamed 'Nosey' – he was, in fact, the original Nosey Parker. He is commemorated in the city by his portrait in **St Peter Hungate** church museum, which also has a copy of the 'Bishop's Bible' – a new translation which he commissioned when he became Archbishop. There is a green plaque in his name on **St Saviour's Church** recording the fact that he was born in that parish and educated in the parish of **St Clement**. In the latter's churchyard you can still see the tomb of his parents.

Ⓜ

PARSLEY, OSBERT (1511–1585)

The only 'singing man' to have his own monument in the **Cathedral**, the wonderfully named Osbert served for 50 years – from 1535 to 1585 – thus spanning four reigns and the turmoil of the *Reformation*. Until Henry VIII's death in 1547 he sang in Latin; during the brief reign of Edward VI the English prayer book was introduced; under Queen Mary it was back to Latin Mass; then the arrival of Elizabeth I saw a return to English.

Osbert sang on, whatever the language and religious climate, and also became a composer. His setting of the Magnificat was sung in the Cathedral when Queen Elizabeth worshipped there in 1578. It must have been the highlight of his long life.

PASTON FAMILY

One of the great families of Norwich, best remembered today for their letters which give such a vivid picture of social life in the 15th century, John and Margaret Paston paid for the rebuilding of the *nave* and *transepts* of **St Peter Hungate** in 1460. They lived within its parish in **Elm Hill** – the family house in which many of the Paston letters were written was purchased by them in 1458 and destroyed in the fire of 1507. It was replaced by a great Tudor mansion built by **Augustine Steward** which still stands.

The Pastons also had property in **King Street**, for it is recorded that Sir John Paston bought the **Music House** in 1488, modified the *Norman* hall and extended the range southwards.

From their house in Elm Hill, the Pastons patronized the nearby **Maid's Head**. It is a tribute to the longevity of both inn and family that, 200 years later, when the Maid's Head was a popular rendezvous for Royalists

Above: St Peter Mancroft.

during the Civil War, the Roundheads descended on it and seized the horse of one Dame Paston.

PASTRY, MR

See **Richard Hearne**.

PEASANTS' REVOLT

See **Geoffrey Lidster**.

ST PETER HUNGATE

The city's church museum since 1936, this attractive little church in Princes Street – the pride of the **Pastons** – was completely rebuilt in the 15th century; the tower and chancel in 1431, the nave and transepts around 1460 and the porch in 1497. On the buttress beside the north door is a carved stone (now protected by glass) on which is depicted the stylized trunk of a tree with the branches cut off but with a leafy sprig growing from the base, symbolizing the decay of the original church and the growth of the new one. It is dated 1460 and was probably placed here by the Pastons.

The interior is a delight, with a superb 'angel' *hammerbeam* roof, broad *Perpendicular* windows, square Norfolk pament tiles on the floor, Norwich-made 15th and 16th century glass in the windows, 'squints' in the transept piers and a holy water stoup beside the north door. There is a particularly good tablet in the west wall to Matthew Goss, a dyer who lived across the street for 60 years until he died in 1779.

The name Hungate was originally Houndgate – the place or street of the dogs. It is believed the Bishops of Norwich kept their hunting dogs in this area.

The contents of the museum are described in more detail under the entry for **Museums**.

ST PETER MANCROFT

Described as the finest parish church in England, this is the largest and grandest of the city's churches and often mistaken by visitors for the **Cathedral**. It was built almost entirely from imported freestone between 1430 and 1455, on the site of a Norman church dating from around 1075, overlooking the **market place** in the parish of Mancroft (thought to be a corruption of Magna Crofta, the great field).

The massive tower houses a famous peal of 12 bells, which rang the first true 'peal' of changes (5,040) in 1715. Inside, the sheer size of the church is staggering; this is no chancel arch to break the view eastwards as eight bays of the aisle arcades march from end to end, while two continuous rows of 16 *clerestory* windows, two to each bay of the nave, are as close to achieving the *Gothic* ideal of a wall of glass as we are likely to see.

The hammerbeam and arch-braced roof is magnificent and the great east window, glowing with 15th-century stained glass, dominates the chancel, which is marked by six suns-in-splendour in the roof above. The west end has a number of items of interest, including a font dating from 1463, a Flemish tapestry of 1573 (chiefly famed for depicting Jesus wearing a hat) and an ancient chest believed to be a unique survivor from the original Norman church.

The north porch has a chamber above it called the Peter Room after an 18th-century sexton, Peter Smyth, who slept there and, in 42 years, dug 2,664 graves.

The mighty tower, double-buttressed at the angles, was probably designed to carry a greater height, as at the famous Boston 'stump' but was never completed. The lead-covered fleche with neat flying buttresses was added in 1895 to make a total height of 145 feet. The parapet and pinnacles date from the same time.

ST PETER PARMENTERGATE

One of two redundant churches in **King Street**, earmarked as a workshop for repairing church organs, this was the parish church of Parmentergate – the place of the leather-workers. It has a handsome west tower and south porch. Inside is the fine Jacobean tomb, erected in 1623, of Richard Berney and his wife Elizabeth. Their praying figures lie under a canopy displaying the Berney and Hobart coat of arms. They had a house in King Street and Elizabeth's father was Edward Hobart of Hales Hall.

(M)

PETTUS FAMILY

From 1550 to 1683 Pettuses inhabited the same house in **Elm Hill**, a small part of which still remains at numbers 41 to 43. The family produced a long list of public figures, including Thomas Pettus (sheriff 1566, mayor 1590) and Sir John Pettus, knighted earlier by Elizabeth I and mayor in 1608.

The male line died out in the 18th century but there are many Pettus descendants in the United States, who make periodic pilgrimages to Elm Hill. It was through the intervention of one American ancestor, at the turn of the century, that **St Simon and St Jude**, the Pettus family church, was saved from demolition.

PIGG LANE

Ambling from **Quayside** to Palace Street, Pigg Lane is a reminder of the old city of Norwich in the days of timber-framed houses, low roofs and narrow cobbled streets. It is thought to have been named after Henry Pigge, one of the constables of Wymer Ward during the Tudor period; he certainly owned property in the lane. An older, 14th century, name is perhaps more appropriate for a street which led to and from the city's main landing stage – Wateryng Lane.

PLAINS

In Norwich a broad area where several streets come together is known as a plain – hence Agricultural Hall Plain, St Martin at Palace Plain, Bank Plain, St Mary's Plain, etc.

POCKTHORPE DRAGON

Towards the end of the 18th century mock-mayoral processions were introduced in imitation of the **Snapdragon** procession which was for centuries an important feature of civic ceremonial. The Pockthorpe Guild, founded in 1772, held its activities on the day following Guild Day. It had its own dragon which led a boisterous procession around the Pockthorpe area – one of the city's poorest districts – with numerous stops at inns for refreshment. Fifty years after the demise of the civic snapdragon in 1850, the Pockthorpe dragon was still roaring around the streets, raising money for charity.

There was a similar tradition outside the city in the village of Costessey (pronounced Cossey). Two Pockthorpe dragons and the head of the Costessey 'snap' still survive in the **Castle** museum. The latter is believed to have belonged at one time to an early civic dragon, which would make it the earliest surviving example of a tradition which was a feature of the city for many generations.

PORT OF NORWICH

Norwich has been a port since its early days. Seagoing vessels could navigate the Rivers Yare and **Wensum** to reach the centre of the city – indeed this was how most of the materials used to build the **Cathedral** were brought to the site. Around 1300 a sand and gravel bar began to form in the estuary at Great Yarmouth and, for around 500 years, sea-going boats could no longer reach the city, although most of the provisions continued to be carried by water in the ubiquitous Norfolk **wherries**.

In 1827 a new channel was cut downstream

of Norwich and other improvements made so that the city became a port again. While pleasure craft far outnumber trading vessels now, seagoing boats continue to visit the city with cargoes of timber, scrap iron, grain and foodstuffs. They can be seen on the stretch of river between **Carrow Bridge** and **Foundry Bridge**. The modern port of Norwich extends 14 miles down river.

POTTERGATE

One of the oldest streets in the city, starting at **St John Maddermarket** and ending at Wellington Lane beside the inner link road, the name is taken from its long association with pottery-making. A number of Saxon kilns have been excavated in this area, including one which gives its name to a modern building, Kiln House, for it was discovered when the foundations of the building were being dug. There were a number of kilns in medieval times between **St Benedict Street** and Pottergate. In addition to domestic pottery, the kilns also produced drainage pipes and bricks. The street extends beyond the inner ring road as West Pottergate.

PRINCE OF WALES ROAD

Constructed in 1860, on the hopfields and orchards which once belonged to the **Austin Friars**, to provide a suitably impressive entry to the city from **Thorpe Station**, it offers some fine examples of mid-Victorian architecture. Prior to its arrival, the main thoroughfare from the station to the city centre was Rose Lane.

PRINCES STREET

Formerly Hungate Street, situated between Tombland and St Andrew's Plain, it offers a splendid variety of ancient buildings and three fine churches – **St George Tombland**, **St Peter Hungate** and the former conventual church of the **Blackfriars** (now **St Andrew's and Blackfriars' Hall**). Sir Nikolaus Pevsner described it as 'one of the best street sequences in Norwich'.

PROSPECT HOUSE

Not all the fine buildings in the city are ancient. The head office of Eastern Counties Newspapers – publishers of the county's daily, evening and weekly newspapers – was designed by Yates, Cook and Darbyshire and opened in 1969 by Princess Alexandra. It stands at the junction of Cattle Market Street and Rouen Road. Norwich has a long and distinguished history of news journals, for the first provincial newspaper in the country, the Norwich Post, was published in the city in 1701.

PUBS

Three hundred years ago it was said that Norwich 'swarmed with ale houses'. In 1838 the city had 27 breweries and 500 pubs – beer cost 1p a gallon! By 1892 the Norwich Gospel Temperance Society listed between 800 and 900. There were more than 20 in the **market place** alone. Only 50 years ago it was the city's boast that it had a pub for every day of the year and a church for every Sunday. Today around 55 pubs still remain within the area of the old city walls, while the names of many streets and tiny courts remind us of inns long vanished.

PULL'S FERRY

Site of the 15th-century watergate – the fourth gate to the **Cathedral** precincts and one of the city's most famous beauty spots – it takes its name from the fact that the river was crossed by ferry at this point from medieval times until as recently as 1943. Traditionally, the ferryman kept a pub next to the gate where he also lived – the 17th-century house is now in private hands. The names of several ferrymen have been handed down to us. An Elizabethan chorister, John Sandlin, was the first to hold the ferry licence granted by

Left: Medieval buildings, Princes Street.

Above: Pull's Ferry and watergate.

Below left: Pykerell's House.

Below: Red Lion Street.

the Dean and Chapter. John Pull (or Poole) was ferryman and publican for 45 years, dying in 1841. The last ferryman was Cecil Mollett, whose father, William, preceded him. The whole of the Pull's Ferry area was restored in 1947/48 by Mr Cecil Upcher, with money raised by local Girl Guides. The Guides serve tea and cakes to the public from Pull's Ferry at weekends during the summer.

PUPPET THEATRE

Well worth a visit for excellent entertainment in an unusual setting, the theatre uses the converted church of **St James Pockhorpe** at the corner of Barrack Street and **Whitefriars**.

Ⓜ

PYKERELL'S HOUSE

Norwich has only five thatched dwellings left – an aftermath of the decision in Tudor times to ban thatch as a roofing material because of the fire risk. This charming late-15th century house in Rosemary Lane, opposite the church of **St Mary Coslany**, is one of them. The home of Thomas Pykerell, three times mayor of Norwich, who died in 1545, it contains a great hall.

~R~

RAILWAY STATIONS

At the start of the railway era, railways were built by private companies which had no powers of compulsory purchase. As a result, they had to buy land for stations wherever they could find a level site at a reasonable cost. For many years the city was served by no fewer than three stations, all built outside the city boundaries in the county of Norwich. They were Thorpe (1844), across the river from **Foundry Bridge**, Victoria (1849) just outside the old **St Stephen's Gate** on the site of the former Ranelagh Pleasure Gardens, and the City Station (1882) on the west bank of the **Wensum** outside the old **Heigham Gate**.

Of the three, only **Thorpe Station** now remains. Incredibly there was once a plan to continue the railway line into the city, terminating at a station near the **Cathedral** close. Happily the Dean and Chapter did not take kindly to the idea.

RAMPANT HORSE STREET

A short length of road between the St Stephens Street/Red Lion Street junction and Theatre Street, named after an inn and yard which once stood where Debenhams is now. This was the place where stallions were displayed for farmers to choose as studs for their mares.

RED LION STREET

Running north to **Castle Meadow** from the junction of St. Stephen Street, Rampant Horse Street and **Westlegate**, Red Lion Street was rebuilt by **George Skipper** between 1900 and 1903 as a result of the introduction of the **tramway** system. It is notable for a fine range of commercial buildings opposite Debenhams store, including Commercial Chambers, Anchor Building (site of the first Norwich night-club before the war) and Standley Livery Stables, with the words stable, livery, forge and shoeing still visible above the entrance. This building has associations with the Norwich vet John Pollock FRCVS, and a ramp for horses can still be seen in the yard. This side of Red Lion Street was fortunate to survive the bombing of the last war when Curls department store opposite was totally destroyed.

REGALIA, CIVIC

Norwich has one of the most outstanding collections of civic plate and insignia of office in the country. Displayed in the Tourist Information Centre in the **Guildhall**, it includes the Crystal Mace, presented to the city by **Augustine Steward** in 1549; the city sword presented by the St George's Company in 1705; and the Meade Salt, the most important piece of Elizabethan plate made by a provincial goldsmith and dating from 1568. The collection is valued at £6.5 million.

There are many other fine items in the collection, some dating from modern times, including a silver model of a sailing ship presented by Spanish schoolchildren and a model – also in silver – of an Overstrand bomber made by a local company, Boulton & Paul.

REGIMENTAL MUSEUM

See **Museums**.

RICHARD II (1367–1400)

This King visited the city in 1383 as part of a royal progress to areas which had put down the Peasants' Revolt. See also **Anne of Bohemia**.

(M)

RIFLEMAN ALE HOUSE

See **Dirty Shirt Club** and **John Crome**

(M)

RIGBY, DR. EDWARD (1747–1822)

Surgeon and apothecary, he studied medicine in Norwich and was associated, at the early age of 24, with the founding of **Norfolk and Norwich Hospital**. He became an expert at operating to remove gallstones (the scourge of Norfolk, then and now), was responsible for introducing vaccination into the city, ran a smallpox hospital and had a licence to keep '12 lunaticks' in a house at Lakenham. He was also the first employer of the young **John Crome**, who discovered his talent as an artist after being fired by Dr Rigby and finding a new job with a signwriter. The house in **St Giles Street** where he was the apothecary's apprentice can still be seen.

Dr Rigby's wife bore him 12 children, the last four arriving as quadruplets when both were already grandparents. The city council were so impressed that they presented him with an inscribed silver bread basket at a cost of £25 – it is not recorded what Mrs Rigby had to say about this. She survived what must have been a horrendous – and normally fatal – ordeal to live into her nineties.

RIOT OF 1272

The great riot between citizens and monks which erupted on 9th August 1272 had its origins in the *Norman* occupation of the city some two centuries earlier. When the seat of the Bishopric of East Anglia was moved from Thetford to Norwich in 1094, Bishop **Herbert de Losinga** laid his plans for a great cathedral church and monastery, started eventually in 1097. Such a massive undertaking required a large amount of space – and it was the old Saxon burgh of **Northwick** which provided it.

The Saxon market place of **Tombland** was placed under the jurisdiction of the priory as the Earl of East Anglia's palace and the church of St Michael – the richest in the city – were swept away to create an open space outside the cathedral gate.

The local people did not take kindly to the

destruction of their homes and churches to make way for a privileged community of foreign monks. The subsequent arrogance, influence and unaccountability of the Benedictine community fanned the flames of resentment for many years to come.

In the 13th century, the monks continued to lay claim to control areas outside their cathedral precincts, including Tombland and **Bishopgate**. Matters finally came to a head at the Trinity Fair in Tombland in the summer of 1272 when a brawl between some of the citizens and the priory servants lit the fuse which led to a full-blown riot. The original spark was the Prior's decision to levy a tax on the fair to meet the Pope's demands for money to finance a crusade. The Prior erected an 'engine of war' on the top of the bell-tower which stood near the present **Erpingham Gate**, presumably to dominate Tombland. The citizens responded by mounting their own device on the tower of the Saxon church which stood opposite, on the site of the present **St George Tombland**, and 'catapulted fire' into the Cathedral grounds. This, followed by a full-scale attack, resulted in the destruction of many wooden buildings plus the more substantial cloisters, a chapel dedicated to St Ethelbert, a nearby gateway and the bell-tower.

It was, however, a pyrrhic victory for the citizens. The King himself, Henry III, then in the last year of his life, had to come to Norwich to restore order, which he promptly did with a violence which stood comparison with what had gone before. The ringleaders were executed by various methods – the favourite seemed to be dragging them to death by horses through the streets – and the citizens were ordered to rebuild the gate with a chapel dedicated to St Ethelbert in its upper storey. This is the present **Ethelbert Gate**, constructed in 1300.

In an early demonstration of the English art of compromise, the priory was granted Bishopgate while Tombland was divided between citizens and monks.

RIVERSIDE WALK

An unusual and very pleasant way to see the city from a different perspective is to take this walk, which follows the banks of the **Wensum** from **Carrow Bridge**, through the heart of Norwich, to Hellesdon, five miles upstream. The idea was first mooted in the 1930s but it wasn't until 1967 that work began to create a suitable pathway and it has continued since then, funded by the city's Amenities Committee with a contribution from the Broads Authority.

ROMAN CATHOLIC CATHEDRAL

See **St John the Baptist**.

ROSARY CEMETERY

A fine example of a Victorian cemetery, now stretching to 13 acres on the hills of Thorpe Hamlet just outside the city. When it was established in 1819, 'on the broad principles of Christian equality' by Thomas Drummond, a retired Presbyterian minister from Ipswich, it was the first private cemetery of its kind in England. Here are buried many of the great personalities of Victorian Norwich – non-conformist merchants, manufacturers, radicals, painters and reformers – and the founder himself, who came to occupy part of his own creation in 1852. It is now under the care of Norwich Corporation. If you like solitude and nature allowed to run riot and old, weathered monuments, this is a place to seek out. The main entrance is in Rosary Road.

ROYAL ARCADE

See **Arcade**.

ROYAL HOTEL

The Royal stands on a triangular site overlooking Agricultural Hall Plain. It is a marvellous example of Victorian monumental architecture, complete with pinnacles, parapets, mullioned windows and ornamental brickwork. It was built with extraordinary speed in 15 months in 1897/98 to a design by Edward Boardman to replace the old Royal Hotel in **Gentleman's Walk**, which was to be rebuilt as the **Royal Arcade**. The building has had a chequered career in recent times. It ceased to offer accommodation in 1977 and became offices for Anglia Television. In 1989 the ground floor was refurbished as a café-bar.

RUSH, JAMES BLOMEFIELD

(1800–1849)

One of the most notorious of 19th-century murderers, he was hanged in public at Norwich **Castle**. Rush shot the Recorder of Norwich, Isaac Jermy, and his son at Stanfield Hall, near Wymondham, in 1848 after Jermy had demanded the prompt return of a £5,000 mortgage loaned to Rush. It is said that Rush planned the murders while drinking in his favourite tavern, the **Adam and Eve**.

~S~

SACK FRIARS

See **Friars**.

SAMSON AND HERCULES HOUSE

Currently suffering under the name of Ritzy's, or something equally inappropriate for such a gracious building, this mid-17th century house opposite the **Erpingham Gate** in **Tombland** takes its name from the huge carved figures which support the portico – Samson carrying a fox and gripping an ass's jawbone, Hercules in a lion's skin, holding a club and performing the first of his labours. The house was built by Christopher Jay, who had the figures carved from wood, painted and enamelled. They stood at the entrance for 132 years until their removal to the inner court in 1789. It was another 100 years before the antique dealer Charles Cubitt found them and returned them to guard the entrance.

The house has had many uses, including a centre for the YWCA (opened by an earlier Duchess of York – now the Queen Mother – in 1924), a swimming-pool and a social centre and dance hall during the war for Allied and American troops; the carved guardians at the door caused the Americans to rechristen it 'Muscles Palace' – a title which at least has the benefit of humour.

It underwent a final restoration in 1952/53 when it was remodelled to its original appearance. It is much older inside than out – parts of it date back to the 12th century and there are *Norman* arches in the basement. It even has a ghost – well, several ghosts; neither Samson nor Hercules but, it is said, a trio of monks.

SANDLIN'S FERRY

See **Pull's Ferry**.

ST SAVIOUR

'A village church that has come to town' is an earlier and apt description of this rustic church in **Magdalen Street**, with its short, squat tower only a few feet from the pavement. The *nave* – much wider than the tower – has more roof than wall and lacks both aisles and *clerestory*. The 14th century *chancel* is

Above and below: George Skipper's terracotta panels, London Street.

lower and narrower than the nave. The east end has an excellent *Decorated* window. There is a porch on the south side which was used as a baptistry in the last century. St Saviour is now redundant and used as a badminton hall. It displays a plaque to **Matthew Parker**, born in the parish.

SHEFFIELD, LORD (1521–1549)

Second-in-command of the expeditionary force sent from London to eject the insurgents from the city during **Kett's Rebellion**. He was killed by Fulke, a butcher, during the battle of St Martin's Plain on 1st August 1549. A plaque on the wall opposite **St Martin at Palace** marks the spot where he fell. He and 35 others who died that day are buried in the church.

SHIRE HALL

Designed by William Wilkins and built between 1822 and 1823 in Market Avenue, this was the scene of the assizes and quarter sessions, and later the crown court, until the opening of the new court complex in **Bishopgate** in 1987/88. Enlarged in 1887 and 1908, and refaced in 1913, it is linked by an underground tunnel with the **Castle** so that prisoners held there could be brought conveniently to trial. Part of the Shire Hall became a new home for the regimental museum of the Royal Norfolk Regiment in 1990.

ST SIMON AND ST JUDE

This is one of only two churches in Norwich with a double dedication – the other is **St Peter Mancroft**, which is dedicated to Saints Peter and Paul. Situated at the junction of **Elm Hill** and Wensum Street, it is a simple flint building of great antiquity – parts of it are thought to have been in existence before the see of East Anglia was moved from Thetford to Norwich late in the 11th century. There are neither aisles nor porches – just *chancel, nave* and a ruined tower. It has two particular features worthy of examination; the broad east window facing Wensum Street with its widely-spaced *mullions* and large *ogees* in the upper part, and the famous **Pettus** monuments on either side of the chancel arch. On the south side, Thomas Pettus, who lived in Elm Hill and was mayor in 1590, kneels in mayor's robes facing his wife, with their family behind. To the north, Sir John Pettus, mayor in 1608, lies uncomfortably on his elbow in full armour, with three of his sons and four of his daughters. The church has been used since 1952 as a Scouts and Guides shop.

SKIPPER, GEORGE (1856–1948)

With the exception of **Thomas Ivory**, no architect has stamped his personality upon Norwich as vividly as George Skipper, who was born in Dereham, educated in the city at Bracondale School and trained at the Norwich School of Art. He was responsible for much of the distinctive architecture of Cromer – the Grand, Metropolitan and Paris Hotels in particular – before turning his attention to Norwich and designing the **Royal Arcade** in Art Nouveau style in 1899. He was equally at home in the Baroque manner, as can be seen in Telephone House in **St Giles** and the magnificent **Norwich Union** head office in Surrey Street.

Much of his work survives in the city, including Jarrolds store in **London Street**/Exchange Street, which incorporated his own office. From London Street you can see, under the first floor windows, a terracotta panel showing details of scenes connected with architecture and building which was designed by Skipper. Today the architectural practice he founded is still designing fine buildings in and around Norwich.

SMITH, SIR JAMES EDWARD (1759–1828)

Born in a house in the **market place**, this

distinguished medical man and botanist purchased the botanical collection of the Swede Carl Linnaeus for £1,000 and formed the Linnaean Society. At his house in Surrey Street he gave lectures in botany and zoology and became a national figure, being knighted for his services to the science of botany. He was one of the leading nonconformists who formed the congregation of the **Octagon** Chapel. Not to be confused with another 18th-century James Smith from the market place, who became the first person to make and sell ready-made shoes – he was a founder of the modern Start Rite shoe company.

SNAPDRAGON

See **Guild of St George** and **Pockthorpe Dragon**

SOANE, SIR JOHN (1753–1837)

Norwich-based architect who designed **Blackfriars Bridge** in 1783 and the gaol at the **Castle** (1789/93) before moving on to higher things and becoming the architect to the Bank of England in the City of London.

DE SOLEMPNE, ANTHONY (d. ? 1606)

Set up the first printing press in Norwich and produced his first book in **Pottergate** in 1572. He later moved his printing works to Dove Street. Ironically one of the pamphlets he printed was a set of verses written by Thomas Brooke on the eve of his execution for plotting to destroy or expel from the city the Protestant **strangers** – of whom de Solempne was one.

SOUTH AFRICAN WAR MEMORIAL

See **Flying Angel**.

SPYNKE, RICHARD (d. ? 1349)

A rich merchant who was responsible for directing the fortifications of the **city gates** between 1337 and 1344 (largely at his own expense) and for building large stretches of the **city walls**. He also provided cannon and ammunition. As a reward for his munificence, he and his successors were freed from further service to the city.

STANNARD, JOSEPH (1793–1830)

Stannard studied under John Crome's friend and colleague, Robert Ladbrooke, and was much influenced by the Flemish masters. His best-known painting, the 'Thorpe Water Frolic', was commissioned by **Thomas Harvey**. It is now in the **Castle** art gallery. Stannard died young of tuberculosis and was survived by his wife, Emily, who was a successful painter in her own right. The Stannards' house at 3, **St Giles Terrace** can still be seen.

ST STEPHEN

While not the greatest of the city's church towers, that of St Stephen in Rampant Horse Street is certainly the prettiest and most unusual, with its patterns of flint and *flushwork* and its location to the north of the main body of the church, attached to the aisle. It is in effect a three-storeyed porch through which one enters the last medieval church to be built in the city, completed after the *Reformation*.

Inside is an excellent hammerbeam roof with angel *corbels* at the eastern end, marking the point where the *rood screen* crossed the nave and aisles. Both east and west windows have fine stained glass and the church is noted for its monuments. Other features to look for include carved *misericords* – believed to be 500 years old – beneath the seats of the choir stalls and a fascinating range of poppy-head designs

Left: Augustine Steward House.

Below: Tombland leading to Ethelbert Gate.

carved on the ends of the pews. St Stephen is a 'live' church and open to the public on Saturday mornings during the summer.

ST STEPHEN'S GATE

See **Nedeham Gate**.

ST STEPHEN'S STREET

Once a narrow winding street leading from the **Nedeham Gate** to the muddy junction of **Westlegate** and Rampant Horse Street, it kept much of its character until the last war when the Luftwaffe began its transformation by destroying the historical thatched Boar's Head public house on the corner of Surrey Street in April 1942.

St Stephen's was widened and modernized after the war and today it is Norwich's premier shopping street, dominated by Norwich Union's 'skyscrapers' on the south side.

(M)

STEWARD, AUGUSTINE (1491–1571)

Described as 'the most active and public-spirited man in the whole city', Steward was the mightiest of the mighty Tudor magnates who ruled Norwich. His devotion to duty and generosity to the city earned him the mayoralty no fewer than three times (1534, 1546 and 1556); he also represented the city as Burgess, or member of Parliament, in 1547.

Every major event in Norwich during his adult lifetime seemed to have his stamp upon it. He directed the rebuilding of the **Guildhall** in 1534 after its collapse; initiated the purchase of the **Blackfriars'** church from Henry VIII in 1540 to provide the city with **St Andrew's Hall**; and was deputy mayor in the critical summer of 1549 when he became the executive in charge of the city during **Kett's Rebellion**, the mayor – Thomas Codd – having fallen into the hands of the rebels. It was Steward's decision to open **St Benedict's Gate** to admit the **Earl of Warwick** and his relieving force that finally turned the tide against the rebels and led to the suppression of the revolt. Having made his fortune as a cloth merchant, Steward was responsible for presenting the silver gilt crystal mace to the city. There is a portrait of this remarkable and energetic man in **Blackfriars' Hall** and two of the houses he built and occupied still stand. See also **Strangers Club** and **Augustine Steward House**.

AUGUSTINE STEWARD HOUSE

Newly built in the year that **Augustine Steward** faced **Robert Kett** and his rebels, this is a famous, half-timbered Tudor dwelling opposite the **Erpingham Gate** in **Tombland** which shows a distinct list to port – a crooked house, indeed. It served as the headquarters for the relieving army of **Lord Northampton** in 1549; Northampton, we are told, 'slept upon cushions and pillows'. After Northampton's defeat by the rebels, Steward retreated to the top floor of the house, from where he could see the city ablaze as the rebels set fire to houses and the **city gates** including **Magdalen, St Augustine's** and **Conesford**. Three weeks later the house again was a military HQ, this time for the army of the **Earl of Warwick**, which defeated Kett's rebels.

The timbers from which Tudor houses were built were often cut to size elsewhere, numbered and then put in position on site. Look at the timbers of the side of the house facing **Tombland Alley** to prove the point. You will find that many of them are inscribed with Roman numerals – an early example of prefabrication.

Augustine Steward House was for a number of years the Tourist Information Centre, which moved to the Guildhall in 1987. Look for Augustine Steward's merchant's mark and initials on the frontage.

STRANGERS

It was to revive the flagging fortunes of the

worsted industry in the 16th century that refugees from the technically advanced textile areas of the Netherlands were invited to Norwich. These strangers – as foreigners were (and are) called in the city – suffered religious persecution at the hands of the Spanish Duke of Alva, for Holland was a Spanish possession at that time, and were glad to seek a more tolerant climate.

There were already 174 refugees in Norwich when the 30 households officially invited by the city authorities arrived in 1565. This trickle turned to a flood and by 1579 there were 6,000 aliens among a total population of 16,000. A century later it was estimated that one in three Norwich inhabitants spoke a foreign language.

The city continued to welcome strangers, including French refugees fleeing religious persecution at the end of the 17th century and others escaping the French Revolution 100 years later. The strangers had their own churches – **Blackfriars** for the Dutch and **St Mary the Less** for the French – and, apart from their weaving skills, they contributed to the city their love of gardens and of canary-breeding, both of which were to become part of the Norwich heritage.

STRANGERS CLUB

Businessmen's club at 22-26, **Elm Hill**, the magnificent house known as Paston Place in the 15th century and rebuilt by Augustine Steward after the fire which devastated Elm Hill in 1507. Steward's merchant's mark and initials can be seen on the great lintel beam to the left of the house.

STRANGERS HALL

See **Museums**.

STUART AND SUCKLING HALLS

Now known as Cinema City, this fine building is not as old as it appears. It was built by Ethel and Helen Colman in 1924 as a concert and meeting hall in memory of their sister, Laura Stuart, at the same time as they restored the adjoining **Suckling House**. The first meeting of the Round Table was held here on 14th March 1927. See also **Louis Marchesi**.

SUCKLING HOUSE

Facing **St Andrew's Hall**, this was originally a city merchant's house built in the mid-14th century; the banqueting hall and arched bays of the kitchen and buttery still remain. The house was occupied in the 16th century by Sir Robert Suckling, twice mayor and member of Parliament. It was in the family for 75 years and was later the home of the Bishop of Durham. It was bought by the Colman family in 1923 and painstakingly restored under the supervision of Ethel and Helen Colman, who returned many historic items removed over the years, including a fine oak door dating from 1510. On 24th October 1925 Suckling House was handed over to the city and declared open by the Duke of York (later George VI).

DE SUFFIELD, WALTER (d. 1257)

Co-founder (with landowner William de Dunwich) and driving force behind the **Great Hospital**, he was born in Norfolk of an old and wealthy *Norman* family, educated at the University of Paris and became Bishop of Norwich. A caring and compassionate man, he once sold the plate off his table to buy food for the poor during a time of grain shortage. When he died on a visit to Colchester, he left a sum of money to be distributed to the poor wherever his body rested on its way to burial.

ST SWITHIN

One of three medieval churches within a few

paces of each other (all redundant) in St Benedict's Street, St Swithin is a plain flint church with a neat little bell turret but no tower (the original was declared unsafe and demolished in 1882). The south side is unremarkable, with an aisle with *Decorated* windows plus *clerestory* windows that are small, square-headed and wide apart, but the north side offers a surprise. Here, running parallel with St Swithin's Alley, is an Edwardian church hall built in *Tudor Gothic* style and as large as the church itself.

The Hall was an unexpected bonus for the Revd. John Sawbridge, who launched an appeal in the opening years of this century to save the church, which had been closed since 1891. An anonymous benefactor, moved by the poverty he saw in the parish, paid not only for the restoration of the church but also for a new social centre where people could meet.

The Edwardian architect responsible, Herbert Green, came up with a building which matches well with the original church, incorporating two flint gables to break the roof line and a large, embattled porch. Both church and hall are now used as an arts centre.

T

THEATRE ROYAL

One of the most successful commercial theatres outside London, it stands in Theatre Street on the site of its two predecessors – the first designed and built by **Thomas Ivory** in 1758 and the second in 1826. The present building dates from 1935. Due to be refurbished in 1990/91, it seats nearly 2,000 and attracts shows and companies from all over the world. It also produces its own shows (including hugely successful pantomimes) and has facilities for making and assembling entire productions.

THORPE STATION

The first Thorpe station was built on open meadowland east of the **Wensum** early in the railway era (1844) as the terminus of the Norwich-Yarmouth line, which was extended to London in 1845. The present station – a prime example of solid Victorian architecture – was built in 1886. See also **Railway Stations**.

TOMBLAND

Nothing to do with tombs or graves – the name comes from the Saxon word 'toma', meaning an open space. Situated between **King Street** and Wensum Street, Tombland was the site of the original Saxon market place and once contained the palace of the Earl of East Anglia and the church of St. Michael, both of which were demolished by the **Normans**, who re-established the centre of Norwich in their own **market place** in the shadow of their **Castle**.

Tombland was also the site of the annual Trinity Fair – a cause of contention between the citizens and the Benedictine monks which led to the great **riot of 1272**. In 1751, Methodism was first preached under the trees of Tombland by the Revd. James Wheatley. As recently as the 1950s, a judgement in the High Court prevented the city corporation from erecting permanent kiosks upon it.

TOMBLAND ALLEY

Tucked away between **Tombland** and **Princes Street**, winding through the churchyard of **St George Tombland**, this alley offers a fine view of the side of **Augustine Steward House**, with its numbered beams and carved wooden shutters, and of the **Erpingham Gate** opposite.

TOURIST INFORMATION CENTRE

See **Guildhall**.

TRAMWAYS

On 30th July 1900 – the last year of Queen Victoria's long reign – the Norwich Electric Tramways Company began to run tramcars (affectionately known as orange boxes on wheels) over 16 miles of 3ft 6in gauge tracks throughout the city.

In its heyday the tram service had a total of 47 four-wheel open-top tramcars in maroon and white livery. Until recently the tram sheds in Silver Road could still be seen – the power station was based in Duke Street.

The arrival and encouragement of petrol-driven motor buses sounded the death knell of the tramway and the last Norwich tramcar made its final journey on 10th December 1935. It was on the Newmarket Road-Riverside service and it was piloted by the company's oldest driver accompanied by its youngest conductor.

Today the only remaining vestiges of that great tramway system are several electricity conducting coils high up on buildings within the city and the reshaping of various streets to facilitate the passage of tramcars. A number of proposals have been made in recent years, however, to initiate a new tramway system as a way to overcome the city's worsening traffic congestion.

~U~

UPPER CLOSE

That part of the **Cathedral** precincts lying to the west of the church, which formed the outer court of the Benedictine monastery. It contains Almary Green, the site of the monastic almonary, a good range of 17th- and 18th-century red-brick houses, the **Ethelbert** and **Erpingham Gates** and statues of **Horatio Nelson** and the **Duke of Wellington**.

UPPER GOAT LANE

See **Lower Goat Lane**.

~W~

(M)

WALLS, CITY

Built between 1297 and 1334 to replace the ditch and bank which had protected the city since 1150, the walls were a colossal undertaking, funded by a tax levied on the citizens thanks to a grant of murage by Edward I. When completed, they stood 20ft high, more than three feet thick and contained 37,000 tonnes of masonry – enough to build 80

Above: Wherry 'Albion' at moorings.

Left: Wherry Tavern sign.

churches at that time. With a ditch 60ft wide and 25ft deep in front of them, Norwich became the largest medieval walled city in the country and in Europe.

In total the walls were some 2½ miles long – the same length as the wall surrounding the City of London – and included bastions, towers and 12 great gates. A wealthy merchant, **Richard Spynke**, supplemented the murage tax out of his own purse to pay for stretches of the wall and most of the gates. The walls were not continuous, however – to the east of the city the authorities relied on the River **Wensum** as a defensive barrier and there was a gap where the river flowed between the **Heigham** and **St Martin's Gates**.

Although the walls were only faced twice by a serious challenge – during the **Peasants' Revolt** of 1381 and **Kett's Rebellion** in 1549 – they served as a means of policing the city, controlling the entry and exit of goods and preventing plague victims and lepers from entering. Eventually the walls outlived their usefulness and fell into disrepair. Unlike York and Dubrovnik, whose solid stone walls have withstood the march of time, Norwich's flint and rubble walls were easy to dismantle and re-use. Today all the gates have gone and only a few stretches of the wall remain, the best being in **Chapelfield** and descending from the **Black Tower** at Carrow Hill.

Ⓜ

WALPOLE, GEORGE (1730–1791)

Walpole inherited the title of Earl of Orford in 1751 and with it the magnificent Houghton Hall, but instead of settling down to the life of a country gentleman, he devoted himself to gambling and the pursuit of pleasure. Most of his exploits bordered on the bizarre, including harnessing four deer to a coach and driving to Newmarket and offering a bet that he could get a flock of geese to London more quickly than a friend could drive a flock of turkeys (Walpole was no fool – he knew that turkeys would roost up trees every night while the geese plodded on).

Despite his nickname of the mad Earl, he became Lord Lieutenant of Norfolk and gave generously to a public appeal to raise money to improve Hog Hill, which was renamed **Orford Hill** in his honour.

He never married but had a succession of mistresses. When his favourite expired, he refused to allow the body to be buried, concealing it under a pile of boots in a cupboard. He died in a way which he would probably have approved of – by falling from his horse while hunting.

WAR MEMORIAL

The city's memorial to the dead of two World Wars stands today in the ornamental gardens in front of **City Hall**. Originally it was placed at the east end of the **Guildhall** and unveiled in 1927 – it was moved to its present site when City Hall was constructed in 1938. The city's ex-servicemen's organizations have been compaigning for another move, this time to turn it round to face City Hall.

WARWICK, EARL OF (1502–1553)

John Dudley, Earl of Warwick, was sent to the city by the Duke of Somerset, Lord Protector for his nephew, Edward VI, to put an end to **Kett's Rebellion** in 1549. Having successfully completed his assignment, Warwick returned to London and staged a coup d'état against Somerset, blaming him for encouraging rebellion through his weakness. Somerset was executed for treason in 1552. Warwick, meanwhile, having confusingly become the Duke of Northumberland in 1551, took control from Somerset but over-reached himself by attempting to place his daughter-in-law, Lady Jane Grey, on the throne in succession to Edward VI. He became the victim of a coup d'état himself and followed Somerset to the scaffold in 1553. His son, Guildford Dudley, and Lady Jane Grey were beheaded a year later.

WATERGATE

A 14th-century gateway to the **Cathedral** precincts spanning the canal which ran from the River **Wensum** until it was filled in during the 1790s. See also **Pull's Ferry**.

WEAVING

The city's main industry from the turn of the 14th century until the Industrial Revolution 500 years later was the weaving of worsted cloth, which took its name from the Norfolk village of Worstead. By the end of the 14th century Norwich was the chief seat of worsted manufacture. In other cloth-making areas, workers were leaving the towns and settling near the fast-flowing streams which turned the fulling mills. This did not happen in Norfolk because worsted cloth did not require the fulling process to clean and thicken it. The skills of the **Strangers** in the weaving of 'new draperies' – light, brightly coloured worsted cloths – led the city into its greatest period of prosperity in the early 18th century. Fifteen Yarmouth ships were permanently engaged in the business of supplying Scandinavia and western Europe with Norwich cloth.

The ingeniously patterned 'Norwich stuffs' were sold as far afield as North America, Russia and the Far East. The resulting prosperity was generally confined to the great cloth merchants, who made large fortunes, rather than the weavers themselves. The success of the Norwich stuffs at home and abroad was based on the fact that Norwich weavers were at times paid 40% less than their main English rivals, the weavers of Exeter serges.

The industry began to decline for a variety of reasons early in the 19th century. The American war of independence, the Napoleonic wars and the demise of the East India Company closed off export markets, while the city could not compete with the machine-made worsted cloths originating in the Midlands and the North, for there were no swift-flowing streams to provide water-power and coal had to be imported from Newcastle for steam-driven machinery.

At one time, 100,000 people throughout the county were concerned in the varied processes of the worsted industry, from raw material to finished garment: yet by 1900 there was not one worsted weaver left in the city.

See also **Yarn Mill**.

WELLINGTON, DUKE OF (1769–1852)

A freeman of the city, the great Duke – hero of the Peninsular War, victor of the Battle of Waterloo and later twice Prime Minister – is commemorated by a statue in the **Upper Close** of the **Cathedral**, near the **Ethelbert Gate**.

This statue and the one of **Horatio Nelson** nearby were originally erected in the **market place** in the 1850s. Nelson was moved to face his old school near the **Erpingham Gate** in 1856 but it was not until 1937, when **City Hall** was being built and the market place rearranged, that Wellington followed. When the statue was moved, coins and newspapers of Wellington's time were found buried beneath the pedestal. These were reinterred on the new site together with coins and newspapers of 1937.

It is appropriate that these two great military heroes should now stand with their backs to one another – they met only once in life and did not get on very well!

WENSUM LODGE

See **Music House**.

WENSUM, RIVER

Without the Wensum, there would probably have been no Norwich, for the city grew out of a number of small settlements established on the gravel terraces on the margins of the river during the Iron Age. The city owed its preeminence in the Middle Ages to the fact that it was the most accessible place in the region

Above: Whitefriars Bridge and Yarn Mill.

Below left: Wild Man tavern.

Below right: Sir Garnet Wolseley pub sign.

to square-rigged trading vessels. The Wensum half encircles the city to the east and north and, in medieval times, it was crossed by five bridges; today there are ten. To the south and east of the city it joins with the River Yare, which eventually drains into the sea at Great Yarmouth. The Wensum is navigable as far as New Mills, a Victorian pumping station which is currently being restored.

The points at which the river can be crossed today are **Carrow Bridge, Foundry Bridge, Bishop Bridge**, Whitefriars Bridge, **Fye Bridge, St George's Bridge** (also known as Blackfriars Bridge), Duke's Palace Bridge, St Miles' Bridge, New Mills and St Crispin's Road. Two excellent ways to explore the Wensum are via the **Riverside Walk** and aboard the steam launch *Princess Victoria*, which is moored just off **Elm Hill**.

WESLEY, JOHN (1703–1791)

Founder of the Methodist Church, Wesley was a regular visitor to Norwich, which in the 18th century embraced non-conformism with considerable enthusiasm. He leased the 18th-century Tabernacle Nonconformist Chapel in **Bishopgate** – designed by **Thomas Ivory** and large enough to seat 1,000 – for six years and had regular confrontations with members of the local Hell Fire Club, who liked nothing better than to disrupt his meetings and beat up Wesley and his followers. The Tabernacle eventually fell into ruins and was demolished in 1953.

A memorial stone to Wesley was dedicated on Wesley Day in 1989; it is situated in the Crown Court gardens near the site of the old Tabernacle in Bishopgate.

WESTLEGATE

Running from **All Saints Green** to the junction of St Stephen's Street and Red Lion Street, Westlegate has been much changed during the course of this century and today only two original buildings – the **Barking Dickey** and **All Saints Church** – remain. The name is probably derived from wastels – white loaves used in religious ceremonies – which were baked in this area.

WESTWICK

One of the four settlements that formed the city in pre-*Conquest* times, probably originating before AD 850 and covering roughly the **St Benedict's**/Westwick Street area. It may have been predominantly a Danish community, and there was evidently some friction with the native inhabitants. The Saxon King Aethelred ordered a purge of the Danes and among those killed was Gunhild, daughter of King Sweyn Forkbeard. In retaliation Sweyn and his Vikings attacked and devastated the settlement of **Northwick** in 1004.

WHERRIES

These great trading vessels were specifically designed to navigate the shallow rivers and broads of Norfolk. The wherry had one great black sail hoisted by a single halliard worked from a small winch at the foot of the mast, wide flaring bows to throw spray away from the foredecks and a shallow draught. When the majority of the city's needs were served via the waterways, the wherries congregated in huge numbers in the city, with dozens of them moored at **Quayside**. It is incredible to think that these great vessels could pass beneath **Bishop Bridge** with their masts lowered flat against the deck. Today the wherry is a thing of the past, with just a few still sailing – thanks to bands of enthusiasts – on the rivers and broads.

WHIFFLERS

City officials – up to six in number – whose role was to walk in front of civic processions to clear the way. In the early years of the 18th century they wore a distinctive costume of scarlet satin breeches, white satin jerkins and a hat decorated with a cockade of feathers and ribbons. They carried swords which they brandished and tossed in the air. Whifflers were assisted by Dick Fools, who wore painted canvas coats with red and yellow cloth caps adorned with fox or cats' tails and small bells. The office was abolished around 1832, but the last Whiffler of Norwich, Joseph Holmes, lived on until 1890 – there is even a photograph of him in his original costume, taken towards the end of his long life.

WHITE FRIARS

The Carmelites or White Friars arrived in the city in 1256 and built their monastery between the site of the present Whitefriars Bridge and the church of **St James Pockthorpe**. The order was dispersed at the *Dissolution*. Some fragments of the monastery are preserved on the site of the modern Jarrolds printing works, including an undercroft and the remains of an *anchorite's* cell.

WILD MAN

The pub next to Hovells basket shop in Bedford Street, the name of which commemorates Peter the Wild Boy, who was found in a German forest, given to King George II and lived for a time in the 18th century in the nearby **Bridewell**, where he was incarcerated as a vagrant, having been found wandering near Rackheath.

ST WILLIAM

A boy said to have been ritually murdered by the Norwich Jewish community in 1144 on **Mousehold Heath** – the Jews were taken into the **Castle** by the sheriff for their own protection, although their complicity in the murder was extremely unlikely. In truth, the boy's death was almost certainly used as an excuse for an anti-semitic riot.

Although he was never officially canonised, William became a figure of veneration locally and a chapel known as St William's in the Wood was founded in the 12th century, near where he died, as a centre of pilgrimage. The chapel was demolished at the *Dissolution* but remnants can still be seen.

WILLOW LANE

A short historic street between **St Giles Street** and **Cow Hill** in the shadow of the churchyard of **St Giles**, Willow Lane is associated with the historian **Francis Blomefield** and the novelist **George Borrow**. It also has a particularly fine Roman Catholic chapel, built in 1827 to a classical design by John Patience, which became a school in 1894 and continued in this role until 1968. Having survived two threats to demolish it since then, the building has been refurbished and converted into a modern office.

WOLSELEY, SIR GARNET

Public house in the **market place** named after the distinguished soldier who re-organized the British Army of which he became Commander-in-chief in 1895. He led the relief of Khartoum but arrived too late to save General Gordon.

~Y~

YACHT STATION

The area of the **River Wensum** between **Foundry Bridge** and **Bishop Bridge** offering mooring facilities for holidaymakers exploring the Norfolk Broads by motor cruiser.

YARN MILL

A superb example of early 19th-century commercial architecture, the Norwich Yarn Company's great mill was designed by John Brown and built 1836–1839 on the site of the medieval Carmelite friary in **Whitefriars**. It stands today as a monument to the decline of the Norwich weaving industry.

The Yarn Mill was built by the Norwich Yarn Company (formed in 1833 by the mayor, Samuel Bignold) in an attempt to counter the fierce competition offered by the thrusting mill masters of Yorkshire and Lancashire, whose machine-made woollen and cotton textiles were produced and sold more cheaply than the 'Norwich stuffs'.

The Mill was sub-let to individual textile manufacturers and held 65 spinning frames and 500 power looms. By 1846 there were 1,700 power looms in the city; in contrast, the West Riding of Yorkshire alone boasted some 25,000. As added difficulties, there were no fast-flowing streams in Norwich to provide water power and coal had to be imported from Newcastle for steam-driven machinery, thus increasing the costs of the finished product.

The Norwich weavers continued this uneven struggle for the rest of the century but the decline was irreversible. Jarrolds – who had started in business in the city in 1823 – took the Mill over in 1902 and today this handsome, ivy-covered building is used by the company as part of their printing works.

See also **Weaving**.

~GLOSSARY OF TERMS~

Anchoress/anchorite
Women and men dedicated to religion who chose to be walled up for life in cells attached to churches. They were very common prior to the Reformation – indeed, Norwich had at least 40 such cells, including one in the ruined (and now vanished) church of St Margaret at New Bridge in St George's Street, which was occupied in 1429 by John Martin.

Apse
Semi-circular end to a chancel.

Arcades
A series of arches supported by pillars down one or both sides of an aisled church.

Basilica
The name given to a church built with a semi-circular or polygonal apse at the east end, a style derived from the original Roman public buildings.

Chancel
Eastern part of a church containing the altar; from the Latin word *cancelli* meaning lattice-work railings. In pre-Reformation times, the chancel was the responsibility of the priest and separated from the body of the church by a screen or railings.

Clerestory
Upper storey of a church, clear of adjacent roofs and pierced with windows which usually correspond with the number of arches or bays in the arcade below. Clerestory windows are usually the principal means of providing natural light in a church.

Conquest
The successful invasion of England by William of Normandy in 1066 which led to the Norman period (1066 to around 1160).

Corbels
Supports set firmly into a wall to carry a weight from above; usually carved decoratively or with heads.

Decorated
A period of marvellously ornate church architecture culminating in reticulated, or net-like, stone tracery and the imaginative use of butterfly and ball-flower motifs. The Decorated period lasted for only around half a century – from 1300 to 1350 – and ended with the catastrophe of the Black Death.

Dissolution
Destruction of ecclesiastical buildings such as monasteries and chantries following the Act of Supremacy of 1535 by which Henry VIII declared himself supreme head of the Church of England. A further wave of despoliation by the Protector Somerset followed Henry's death in 1547 and the ascension of the boy King, Edward VI.

Early English
The first really native English style of church architecture, spanning the period 1200 to 1300.

Flushwork
Use of knapped flints set flush into panelled patterns of stone or brick to give a striking visual effect.

Gothic
Term devised in the last century (and used initially in a derogatory sense) to describe the pointed arch style of church architec-

ture which pertained throughout Europe from the 12th to the 16th century.

Hammerbeam

Late 15th/early 16th century concept by which the thrust of a church roof's weight is taken on 'hammer' brackets or beams. The ends of hammer beams are often embellished with angels or decorative mouldings.

Misericord

Ledge or bracket on the underside of the seats in choir stalls to support the aged or infirm during long periods of standing. From the Latin word for pity.

Nave

Main body of a church, from the western end to the chancel rail. Originally the part of the church for which the congregation were responsible. From the Latin word *navis* meaning ship; it is believed that the early wooden church structures reminded the worshippers of an upturned boat.

Norman

The historical period from the invasion by the Norman French in 1066 to around 1160.

Ogee

Flowing 'S' shaped arch or moulding – a convex curve flowing to a concave one. A favourite of stone masons during the Decorated period.

Palimpsest

A memorial brass which has been used again by turning it over and engraving on the reverse. From the Greek *palimpsestos* (*palim*, again; *psao*, rub smooth).

Perpendicular

Style of architecture of the majority of Norwich's medieval churches. It lasted for some 200 years – from around 1350 to 1560 – and is characterized by soaring upward lines of vertical mullions in huge windows, majestic towers, meticulously panelled buttresses and the ornamented bases of walls.

The main importance of the Perpendicular style is that it was relatively straightforward for inexperienced men to interpret following the death of many of the skilled stone masons in the great plague of 1349 (the Black Death), in which half the population of Norfolk and Suffolk is believed to have perished.

Rebus

Representation of a name in a carving or drawing – a kind of visual pun. In the Cathedral, Bishop Lyhart's rebus is a hart lying in water, while Bishop Goldwell's is a well-head painted gold.

Reformation

By the Act of Supremacy of 1535, Henry VIII declared himself supreme head of the Church of England, over which he exercised dictatorial powers. Confirmed by the Six Articles of Religion in 1539, he upheld the Catholic faith in everything except the supremacy of the Pope. The old Catholic liturgy and rites were wholly maintained throughout his reign. His daughter, Mary Tudor, restored communion with Rome and the rites and furnishings of the Catholic faith but her successor, Elizabeth I, who came to the throne in 1558, re-established the independence of the Church of England, with herself as supreme governor, declaring the church to be Catholic but reformed.

Reredos

Painted or carved screen at the back of an altar.

Rood beam

Pre-Reformation, a loft, platform or beam stood above the rood screen, on which was placed a crucifix with images of the Virgin and St John the Evangelist on either side. Such beams were removed on the instructions of Elizabeth I and few can now be seen.

Rood screen

Wooden carved screen stretching from pillar to pillar under the chancel arch which, prior to the Reformation, separated the clergy's chancel from the people's nave. A large number of screens still survive in Norfolk churches.

Spandrel
Triangular space between the curves of an arch, or the supporting braces of a roof, often filled with carvings or tracery.

Transepts
Where a church has been built in the shape of a cross, the transepts are the short 'arms' to the north and south.

~SELECTED BIBLIOGRAPHY~

A large number of books, leaflets and newspaper cuttings were consulted during the compilation of this guide. The following is a necessarily limited list which should allow the reader to pursue further any of the entries about which he or she would like to know more. Most of the publications are available from the Tourist Information Centre, Guildhall, Norwich, although it should be noted that a number of them, mainly those with no publisher listed, are currently out of print.

Ayres, Brian: **Digging under the Doorstep/Digging Deeper,** Norfolk Museums Service, 1987

Bell, T.: **On the Ball, City,** Wensum Books, 1972

Broads Authority and City of Norwich: **Norwich Riverside Walk,** 1985

City of Norwich Amenities: **Norwich Official Guide,** 1989

Condon, E.: **King Street, A Guided Walk,** King Street Publications, 1983

Dunn, I and Sutermeister, H: **The Norwich Guildhall,** City of Norwich (undated)

Eastern Counties Newspapers: Various articles, **Eastern Daily Press** and **Eastern Evening News**

Farrant, A.: **A History of the Maid's Head Hotel,** 1975

Gardiner, R.: **The Story of Norwich Cathedral,** The Dean and Chapter of Norwich Cathedral, 1987

Goreham, G.: **Norwich Heritage** (Vols 1 and 2), F. Crowe & Sons Ltd., 1981

Green, B.: **Norwich Castle, A Fortress for Nine Centuries,** Jarrold & Son Ltd., 1970

Green, B. and Young, R. M. R.: **Norwich, The Growth of a City,** Norwich Museums Service, 1981

Hoare, A.: **In Search of Robert Kett,** A & A. Hoare (undated)

Horsfield, B. R. and Habgood, D. J.: **A Walk Around Old Norwich,** 1981

Howes, L.: **Illustrated Guide to Elm Hill,** Jarrold & Son Ltd., 1983

Jarrold Colour Publications: **Admiral Lord Nelson** (undated)

Jarrold & Son Ltd: **Historic Norwich,** 1981

Jewson, C. B.: **History of the Great Hospital, Norwich,** The Great Hospital, 1980

McFadyen, Revd. P.: **Edith Cavell 1865–1915, A Norfolk Heroine,** 1982

McLean, M.: **St Julian's Church and Lady Julian's Cell,** 1981

Norfolk Museums Service: **The Norwich Snapdragon,** 1984

Norfolk Museums Service: **Strangers Hall Museum,** 1980

Norwich Tourist Association: **Norwich City Pub Trails** (undated)

Norwich Tourist Association: **Old Churches of Norwich** (undated)

Rose, E. J.: **The History of Mousehold Heath** (undated)

Sansbury, E.: **An Historical Guide to Norwich Cathedral,** The Dean and Chapter of Norwich Cathedral

Sharp, Revd D. M.: **The Church of St Peter Mancroft, Norwich,** Jarrold Colour Publications, 1978

Solomons, C.: **Plaques of Norwich,** Capricorn Books, 1981

Spencer, N.: **The Old Churches of Norwich,** Jarrold & Son Ltd., 1970

Sutermeister, H.: **The Norwich Blackfriars,** City of Norwich, 1977

Young, R.: **Norwich Discovery Walks,** The Norwich Society, 1983

Young, R. M. R.: **Guide to the St Peter Hungate Church Museum,** Norfolk Museums Service, 1975